AN IDENTIFICATION GUIDE TO

TREES

OF BRITAIN

and North-West Europe

Dominic Couzens
and Gail Ashton

T0347136

JOHN BEAUFOY PUBLISHING

First published in the United Kingdom in 2024 by John Beaufoy Publishing Ltd
11 Blenheim Court, 316 Woodstock Road, Oxford OX2 7NS, England
www.johnbeaufoy.com

Photo Credits
Front cover: Weeping Willow © Gail Ashton
Back cover, top to bottom: Rowan berries; Aspen leaf; Giant Sequoia cones
all © Gail Ashton

Photo credits:
All photographs by Gail Ashton except:
Dominic Couzens: p.35 top right, p.37 top, p.154 top right.
Bob Gibbons: p.7 top, p.27 left, p.29 top right, p.32 left, p.42, p.43, p.45, p.48,
p.49 bottom, p.55 bottom, p.62, p.72 bottom right, p.91 top left, p.94, p.95, p.107
bottom left, p.110, p.125 bottom right, p. 131 bottom, p.135 bottom, p.136 bottom
centre, p.140 top, p.144 bottom left, p.151 bottom

Great care has been taken to maintain the accuracy of the information
contained in this work. However, neither the publishers nor the authors can be
held responsible for any consequences arising from the use of the information
contained therein.

ISBN 978-1-913679-45-3

Edited by Krystyna Mayer
Designed by Nigel Partridge
Project management by Rosemary Wilkinson
Printed and bound in Malaysia by Times Offset (M) Sdn. Bhd.

CONTENTS

INTRODUCTION

The Trees in this Book   4

Identifying Trees   4

Taking it Piece by Piece   5

A Year of Trees   9

Glossary   11

Notes on Species Descriptions   11

SPECIES DESCRIPTIONS

Gingkos   13

Monkey Puzzle   14

Yews   16

Cypresses & Junipers   18

Pines   24

Willows & Poplars   38

Walnuts   56

Bog Myrtles   58

Birches & Hazels   60

Beeches & Oaks   70

Elms   80

Mulberries   84

Magnolias   85

Laurels   87

Planes   88

Myrtles   90

Rose Family   92

Maples   118

Pea Family   126

Rhododendrons   127

Hollies   128

Spindles   130

Dogwoods   132

Boxes   134

Buckthorns   135

Oleasters   138

Mallows   140

Olives & Lilacs   146

Moschatels   152

FURTHER INFORMATION   158

INDEX   159

ACKNOWLEDGEMENTS   160

INTRODUCTION

The aim of this book is to help readers identify the trees around them, whether they live in a town, city or the countryside. It is intended to be simple, helping those who might be making their first steps towards tree identification. It should also help readers to appreciate and understand trees a little more.

THE TREES IN THIS BOOK

Rather than being comprehensive, this book only includes species that you are likely to encounter – to see the wood for the trees, if you like. Many tree-identification books, even those intended just for Britain, include a good 300 species. These include not only native species, but also a wide range that arrived in the region as part of collections from all over the world. Some introductions, such as rhododendrons, are as familiar as any native trees and are commonly found in the countryside and parks. Others are much more obscure. The picture is greatly complicated where similar trees to the region's native ones have been introduced, such as the Turkey Oak from eastern Europe, which is different from and needs to be distinguished from, Britain's 'own' oak species. The addition of these trees makes everything more complicated, for both a would-be tree identifier and a tree-book compiler.

Another problem is that people will not leave trees alone. They nurture them, get curious about them, and hybridize and crossbreed them, and the results can be seen everywhere. This can lead to the situation in which a hybrid becomes a dominant tree. Indeed, the most common lime in the region, the 'Common Lime', is a hybrid, and the Grey Poplar, another hybrid, is the most common in much of Britain. Parks and gardens are littered with choice cultivars, and while many of them are glorious, they do add to the range of plants that anyone could come across. This is, though, a delightful problem to have. Throughout the region there is so much to enjoy, to get your teeth into. Trees are truly amazing.

You have to start somewhere, though, to identify so many tree species accurately. This guide thus includes just under 100 species. They include trees and shrubs that you might find in the wild or growing in your local park or open space. The selection does not pretend to be comprehensive, but the most common native species are included, and most of the others are either very common in cultivation or naturalized (such as magnolias), or very distinctive (like the Monkey Puzzle tree). The book stands or falls on the selection, but it will never be perfect.

There is one seemingly obvious question to answer – what exactly is a tree? And what is a shrub, or bush? Without exception, all trees and shrubs have woody stems and the growth is added to every year. Trees are defined as having a single main stem of 5m or more in height, while shrubs are lower and might have many stems.

IDENTIFYING TREES

In some ways, identifying trees ought to be straightforward. After all, they do not run or fly away as do birds or insects, but just stand there waiting for you to pronounce on them. It should be simple, except – it is not.

One big problem with trees and shrubs is that individuals do not necessarily look the same or represent their species in a consistent way. By contrast, imagine a Blue Tit or a ladybird species. Almost every individual of a Blue Tit looks consistently like a Blue Tit, and even birds with different seasonal plumages tend to look similar – it is part of the way they interact. Insects are similar, and this also applies to their early stages – a ladybird larva tends to look much like another larva of the same species.

This consistency applies to trees and shrubs much less. One Pedunculate Oak tree can look completely different from another of the same age. This is partly down to natural individual variation, which is far more obvious than it ever is in, for example, birds. Trees have different heights, lengths and directions of branches, and myriad other differences. These are dependent on soil conditions, shade conditions, competition, human activity, browsing history, insect-predator history, drought, rain and frost, all of which can contribute to variety even within a species. Obviously, many characteristics, such as leaf and flower shape, are inherited, but what this means is that trees are harder to pin down immediately than are birds, mammals or even insects such as butterflies.

So, with trees, the rules are slightly different. The best way to identify them is to cut them down into parts – not literally, of course. Take a note of whatever is on the tree, whether that is leaves, twigs, buds or flowers. The more carefully you examine a tree, the more likely you are to identify it. Few people can simply look at every tree and know what it is. You have to start piecemeal. This guide therefore includes as many recognizable parts of each tree species as possible.

One quick note about recognition: trees are easily divided into two categories, which are technically known as gymnosperms and angiosperms. Do not let the names put you off, because most people know them as conifers and broadleaved trees, or coniferous and deciduous trees. In practice, it is easy to tell them apart. Conifers have needle-like, thin leaves, which are dense and usually evergreen, and they also produce woody cones. Broadleaved trees have, as their name implies, much broader leaves. Usually, broadleaved trees shed their leaves in autumn (this is what deciduous means) and regrow them in spring, although there are some exceptions to these general rules.

TAKING IT PIECE BY PIECE

Leaves These are the most abundant parts of a tree, and all trees have them. However, many trees only have them for part of the year. They all have the same function – to create food by converting the sun's energy into sugars, by a chemical reaction known as photosynthesis. Conifers and other evergreen trees can photosynthesize all year round, but most broadleaved trees concentrate their photosynthesis in spring and summer and shut down their growing season when the days get shorter. The green chlorophyll is withdrawn from the leaves and, before they fall, they often turn into glorious shades of yellow, red or purple.

Leaves are often very distinctive. In fact, you could probably identify every tree in this book just by the leaves if you looked carefully enough. There are books that give you keys to do just that, if you have the patience. They are always a good guide.

Leaves do vary in size, even within an individual tree. They even vary considerably in shape – early leaves may look different from late leaves, and the leaves of suckers (shoots that spring from the underground roots of the same tree) may also look different.

Austrian Pine

Field Maple

There are many things to look for in leaves: size, shape, the nature of the veins, whether they have teeth, how lobed they are, whether they are in pairs along the stem (opposite) or alternate, how hairy they are, how symmetrical they are and how long their stalks are – all good fun.

Trunk & Branches The trunk and branches are the essence of a tree, and they are, at least, always visible throughout the year. They can be of great help in identification, but there is only so much a tree can do with its trunk, and the variety is not as great as you might think.

Some trees have distinctive bark, such as the white of a Silver Birch tree or the subtle purple of a Wild Cherry. Eucalypts are easy to recognize, as are London Planes, both having peeling bark. Some trees have smooth bark, such as Beeches, while others have very rugged bark; older Sweet Chestnut trees often look as though some giant hand had twisted their bark. However, bark is subtle and highly variable. Most trees start out smooth and become rugged with age, just as the skin of humans does.

Another set of a tree species' characteristics involves the shapes of branches. They might point upwards, something taken to extremes in a Lombardy Poplar, for example, or be rather horizontal. Some tree branches arch over. There may be differences in how they twist and divide. Some, such as the Common Lime, are easy to identify because there is almost always a nest of twiggy shoots at the base. Another feature to check is the height of the bole of a tree (the bole is the part of the trunk below the first branches). Some trees also naturally grow higher than others, and their majesty or modesty is a feature in itself.

Flowers The flowers of a tree are the reproductive parts. Here there is a major distinction between gymnosperms (conifers) and angiosperms (the rest).

The idea behind reproduction is to get the male pollen to the female ovary. This can be from different trees or, as a short cut, from the same tree.

In the case of gymnosperms, you could envisage it as transferring from one kind of cone to the other. Male 'cones' are produced in spring and emit pollen in vast quantities; it is released directly from sacs on the soft scales of the male cones. The pollen drifts on the wind, sometimes in clouds, until it reaches female cones; once the pollen is released the male cone is shed. The big difference between conifers and the rest is that the female part, the ovule, the forerunner of the seed, lies naked on the scale of the soft, newly produced female cone, whereas in angiosperms the seed is confined within a fruit. As soon as fertilization occurs, the female cones shut and mature, becoming

Silver Birch

London Plane

Sweet Chestnut

European Larch

Tree reproduction is somewhat more complicated than described above, and there are several categories of lifestyle that are worth mentioning. In some species, male and female parts are found on separate trees, and are described as dioecious. Their strategy is somewhat risky, as the pollen must be transferred to another individual tree. Other trees have separate flowers, but on the same tree (monoecious). This is a good safety net but not so good for genetic variation. Still other trees have male and female parts within the same flower; many of these can self-seed, but others require pollen from another individual to fertilize properly.

Fruits & Seeds Fruits are the fruits of reproductive labour, proof that fertilization, in all its myriad forms, has taken place. Not surprisingly, fruits form later in the season than flowers, and they quite naturally arise from the fertilized female part of the flower. In the case of catkins, they simply go brown and might elongate, but look quite similar to what has gone before. However, in most trees, fruits look very different from flowers. Fruits contain seeds, and the latter are sometimes called nuts. There may

Blackthorn

woodier, and eventually ripen to release the seeds directly.

Tree flowers vary quite a bit, largely according to how they are pollinated. Some are wind pollinated, others insect pollinated, and their flowers reflect this – the showier they are, the more likely that their function is to attract insects. Many wind-pollinated trees have hanging flowers called catkins, which are heads of many individual flowers. Most of them produce catkins early in the year, allowing their pollen to sweep around the canopy unfettered by leaves. Good examples are Hazel, willows, birches and poplars. All these trees produce female catkins, too, to lap up the pollen, although many female flowers are much smaller than the male flowers.

Many species of well-known trees, such as oaks, beeches and Hornbeams, produce surprisingly unremarkable flowers that are easy to miss. However, other trees mass produce their flowers as if they were trying to stage their own personal festival. Masses of flowers on trees are usually referred to as blossom, and blossom is one of nature's great delights. Many trees produce blossom early, taking something of a chance on the weather being kind to potential pollinators, while others wait until much later. The season of a blossom can be a clue to a tree's identity (p. 9).

Pedunculate Oak

Sea Buckthorn

be just one seed in a fruit such as an oak acorn, or sometimes just two, as in the case of a Sweet Chestnut, but sometimes there are many. Fruits are often easy to identify, as shown by their local names, such as acorns (oaks), mast (Beech) or keys (Ash). Many are berries, which can be identified by their colour and texture (and we can eat many of them ourselves).

Fruits are superfluous unless they can get the seed to a piece of fertile ground, where it can germinate, and in most cases, trees want their seeds to be dispersed some way away from the parent tree. Apart from a few unusual cases, such as alder seeds being dispersed by water, trees rely on the wind, or a vector such as a bird or mammal. Some wind-dispersed trees, such as maples and Sycamores, have special aerodynamic, winged seeds, called samaras, which helicopter their seeds away, or they have leafy bracts to give them a lift, as in the case of limes. Still others rely on their seeds being light, although even these, such as birch seeds, still have small flaps like wings.

Animal vectors eat the flesh of the berry and, if all goes well, they spit out the seed or it goes through their gut and is excreted far away from the parent tree. Many animals, however, eat seeds as well as berries, and these are known as seed predators.

Dispersal is an extraordinarily haphazard process.

No wonder many trees live such a long time, to ensure that they successfully reproduce even once in an uncertain world.

Shoots, Buds & Suckers Many trees can be identified by other parts, such as the woody twigs, the newly growing twigs, the shoots, or the buds, which are the forerunner of twigs, leaves or flowers.

Shoots can be identified by their shapes, such as how straight they are, and also by their colour. Dogwood is famous for its red shoots that are obvious in the bare winter landscape. Lime trees have red twigs. Buds are the packages of anticipation. It is quite a skill to identify them, but just

Common Beech

about every tree has identifiable buds and there have been books written about this single subject. Most specifics are outside the range of this book, but some pointers are provided. A few trees, such as beeches, have readily identifiable buds.

Some trees cannot be fussed with all that reproductive nonsense and eschew the dating game altogether by sending up new shoots from their own roots. These are known as suckers, and they can quickly take over an area, or even form their own woodland in the case of the Aspen. The problem is that these growths are vulnerable because there is no genetic variation. But as dense bushes of Blackthorn attest, it can be a very effective form of spreading.

A YEAR OF TREES

One of the many great delights of trees is that there is not a single day of the year when there is not something marvellous to see – and trees create atmospheres, and feelings. They always have. Even in the depths of winter, tree-lovers can enjoy trying to recognize bark, and there are buds everywhere – gift-wrapped promises of better times ahead. Trees aren't just organisms. They are habitats, alive or dead. Living things – be it a bird, an insect or a fungus – depend on trees to survive. And we need them, too, for a multitude of uses, not least for carbon capture – and our future.

January is a season when some trees come into their own. The white bark of birches is obvious in the dull landscape. Alder is red and Dogwood twigs shine crimson. Willows often look yellow, and the towering branches of poplars look even more unreachable than they do in summer. Conifers green the landscape and their shapes come to the fore. However, perhaps January belongs most to the Hazel, which is already producing catkins, even if they are not ripe yet. Each catkin is a flag of bunting to dispel winter gloom.

February heralds the arrival of the first blossom, usually in the suburbs, where Cherry Plum is the cheery plum. The first magnolias form their living candlesticks, ready to hand their blooms to the early pollinators. Alder is already colourful, its dense branches busy with its two-step of cones and catkins.

By the month's end the first willows may blossom, but this is usually a feature of **March**. Pussy willows, which are unopened buds that are white and furry like the paws of a cat, suddenly burst into miniature wigs of yellow stamens. Blackthorns flower as if they were billionaires trying to get rid of all their money at once, their blooms such a riot that they can make it look as though snow is covering the landscape. Poplars are equally profuse with their catkins. Black-type poplars and aspens chuck off spent red catkins like unwanted socks, so that they litter the ground.

April is an arboreal whirr. Almost every tree is throwing something out, and the countryside is fit to burst. It explodes with a thousand greens, every single green the quintessence of freshness, and it throws out blossom, the living snow of petals, the confetti of the wild. Humans love blossom, and it is given in abundance by a succession of different species at different times, Pears before apples, for example, and Wild Cherry before Bird Cherry. There is pink blossom and white blossom, as perfect as a bride's dress, and there is cream blossom that you would love to pour over your chocolate cake.

May is the month of, well, May blossom, as the Hawthorn's is called. Many other trees and shrubs are producing all sorts of flowers, from the opulent candelabras of Horse Chestnuts to the subtle spikes of Buckthorn and the green lace curtains of oaks. And everywhere, there are leaves. The countryside completes its transformation.

By **June**, fresh green seems to have turned to a sort of working green, as trillions of leaves photosynthesize. Canopies fill up – beech canopies are closed to the public, and nothing grows beneath them, even some of their own leaves. Other canopies are delightfully open, such as those of birches. The canopies of lime trees, with their lemon-and-lime flowers, rain down honeydew from happy aphids drinking sap. This is the first obviously humming month, when almost every part of a wood is filled with insects, flying and busy.

July sees the first transitions from the heady days of reproduction to the harder working days of childcare. Untold numbers of fertilized seeds lurk. The first to fruit are usually cherries, those hanging

Weeping Willow

delicacies that are usually found by birds that are themselves immersed in looking after young.

August can seem a tired month. Most flowers have served their purpose and the leaves, too, are on borrowed time. But the 'berries' have begun, in all their forms, from the perfect and lethal red lights of the Yew to the smorgasbord of the Wayfaring Tree and Alder Buckthorn.

By **September**, fruits are springing out everywhere, Rowan on upland moors and Holly on woodland edges. A few leaves, such as those of birches, begin to change colour. It is a season of yellowing, as well as mellowing.

By **October** everyone notices trees, whether they are fruiting or changing colour. Everywhere berries are produced en masse, the wild equivalent of supermarket shelves, ready for their customers, be they birds by day or, often, mice and other mammals by night. The berries are sometimes well known enough to have their own names – haws of hawthorns, sloes of Blackthorn – and some, such as the Juniper and even the Wild Service Tree have their own alcoholic drinks – to say nothing of apples, pears and plums.

November is falling time, for leaves and fruits. Sweet Chestnuts turn the ground prickly and fill ovens everywhere. Conkers from Horse Chestnuts find their way to school playgrounds. Acorns drop and beechmast falls, the latter a sublime autumn harvest so important that it can determine a bird's population the next year. The seeds of maples and Sycamores do not fall as much as fly to the ground, propelled by winged seeds, while those of limes and hornbeams hitch a lift on strange, leafy bracts. Meanwhile, leaves turn to colour so extraordinary and glamorous that we can but look on in awe. Maples often steal the show. Spindles produce fruits so ridiculous that they look like exotic sweets from upmarket shops.

December is a month of fallen leaves and faltering day length. Holly becomes a celebrated tree, for its long-lasting red berries and evergreen leaves, the prickles forgiven. After months of tree activity, it becomes a little quieter, although down in the depths, some seeds have found fertile ground, against the odds, and will be part of the story in years to come. Other trees will see their hundredth, even thousandth Christmas. And everywhere, if you care to look, there are buds. Buds are like fireworks ready to be lit, and they are waiting.

GLOSSARY

As far as is feasible, technical terms have been avoided, but some important terms are explained below.

angiosperm Referring to broadleaved or deciduous trees. Seeds contained within a fruit.

aril Fleshy covering of a seed.

bole Trunk of a tree.

conifer Tree that has needle-like, thin leaves, which are dense and usually evergreen, and also bears cones; often a general term for gymnosperms (see below).

conker Seed of a Horse Chestnut.

coppice Method of forestry in which a tree is cut down to its stumps at ground level after a few years, to encourage new growth.

corolla Totality of petals in a flower.

corymb Flat-topped flower cluster, in which the outer flowers come out first.

cultivar Variation of a formerly wild plant produced in cultivation by any number of propagation techniques.

cupule 'Cup' made up from flower bracts that hold the nut.

cyme Flat-topped flower cluster, in which the outer flowers come out last (see also corymb).

deciduous Refers to tree that drops its leaves during part of the year, usually autumn, leaving bare branches and twigs.

dioecious Species of tree in which male and female trees are separate individuals.

drupe Fruit containing a stone (i.e. a seed).

gymnosperm Referring to conifers (see p. 6).

introduced Refers to plant or animal that has been brought to a place artificially by people, sometimes accidentally, usually intentionally.

key Hanging seed of an Ash and some other trees.

monoecious Refers to species of tree in which male and female flowers are on the same plant.

native Refers to tree that occurs in a place naturally.

naturalized Refers to tree that has been introduced to an area, and has entered the wild state, outside the direct influence of people.

needles Narrow leaves of some coniferous trees.

panicle Spike of flowers radiating from a central stem.

pollarding Pruning system in which branches are cut well above ground, allowing for new growth to sprout from the cut sections.

pome Fruit produced by trees in the apple family. It has a central core containing multiple seeds surrounded by soft flesh.

raceme Spike of stalked flowers radiating from a central shaft.

samara Winged fruit.

spreading Refers to trees with considerable horizontal as well as vertical branches.

stamen Male parts of a flower (a stalk plus an anther).

style Female parts of a flower.

sucker Shoot that grows from a root or base of a tree.

NOTES ON SPECIES DESCRIPTIONS

The months highlighted in the calendar at the top of the page indicate when the leaves, flowers and/or fruits might be seen but these are a guide only.

leaves	cones
flowers	male cones
fruit	female cones

 Identification features of the species, including trunk, leaves, bark, shoots, flowers, cones and fruits as relevant.

 Life history of the tree, including information on pollen, seeds and their dispersal as well as the life span of the species.

 Describes the uses to which the whole tree or parts of it can be put.

 Fascinating facts about featured species.

On the distribution maps, green indicates where the trees grow naturally, dark red where the tree has been introduced, for example in parks, streets and gardens. The area covered includes Britain, Ireland, northern France, Belgium, the Netherlands, Luxembourg, northern Germany, northern Poland, the Baltic States, Scandinavia and Finland. Iceland is not included.

JAN	FEB	MAR	APR	MAY	JUN	JUL	AUG	SEP	OCT	NOV	DEC

MAIDENHAIR TREE

Ginkgo biloba

Had this book been written 200 million years ago it would have been full of *Ginkgo* species. These spiky, branched trees with their unique leaves are dominant in the fossil record for that time, but they declined and eventually all but died out, leaving just the single species. It is quite possible that there are no surviving wild trees left, but the Maidenhair Tree is common throughout the world in cultivation and is famously long lived and tolerant of pollution. It is a large tree with

Planted in parks and gardens and on street corners. Widespread.

a spiky tree, often leans

ABOVE LEFT & RIGHT: *THE TREE IN SUMMER AND WINTER*

FACT FILE

FAMILY Ginkgoaceae (Ginkgos) HEIGHT Maximum 50m SIMILAR SPECIES None.

a narrow crown, to 35m, looking spiky with short side shoots, and often leans.

LEFT & ABOVE: *UNIQUE FAN-LIKE LEAVES*

 Easily identified by the leaves, which are unique and unlike the leaves of any other tree. **LEAVES** Delightful fan shapes, each with a notch in the middle, turning glorious yellow in autumn; 10–12cm long, 7cm wide. **BARK** Distinctive, corky, craggy and somewhat silvery. **SHOOTS** Two forms. The haphazard shape of the tree is due to two forms of shoot: long, horizontal ones that bear short ones crowded with leaves. **FLOWERS** Male tree bears yellow catkins, female tree a single green knob, in late spring. Both are easy to miss among the leaves. Male catkins 2–4cm long; female catkins 4mm long and oval.

 Male and female trees are separate. **SEEDS** White nuts, fertilized by swimming sperm moving from the pollen to the ovule. **FRUITS** Yellowish and plum-like. **LONGEVITY** At least 1,000 years.

BELOW: *GREYISH, CORKY BARK*

You could find yourself exercising your brain on a chess board made of Ginkgo wood.

Six trees in the Japanese city of Hiroshima grew only 1–2km from the site of the nuclear blast in 1945 but survived and are still living today.

JAN	FEB	MAR	APR	MAY	JUN	JUL	AUG	SEP	OCT	NOV	DEC

Planted for decoration. Introduced from South America.

MONKEY PUZZLE

Araucaria araucana

The delight of the Monkey Puzzle tree is that it looks so strange and otherworldly that you can truly imagine it being grazed in prehistoric times by long-necked dinosaurs, which is almost certainly what happened. Its unique branches and leaves are unmistakable, and most individuals look as though they need to have their hair combed.

Very easy. This is a tall, bare-trunked tree with swirling branches, to 30m in height. **LEAVES** Unique (as is the largely bare cylindrical trunk). They are leathery, hard, sharp tipped, triangular and arranged in spirals along the branches; 3–5cm long. **BARK** Corky, knobbly and thick, marked by rings. **CONES** Male cones orange and oblong; 10–12cm long. Female cones 12–20cm

RIGHT: *LEAVES IN SPIRALS*

male cones oblong shaped

long, taking two years to ripen. Female cones heavy, globe shaped and spiny.

 Male and female cones usually grow on different trees. **SEEDS** (Nuts) remain attached to cone scale and drop from cone. **LONGEVITY** 1,000 years plus.

 Fruits are edible.

 Each of the leaves lives for about 24 years.

BELOW LEFT: *KNOBBLY BARK*

BELOW RIGHT: *FEMALE FLOWER*

unique 'badly combed' shape

FACT FILE

FAMILY Araucariaceae (Monkey Puzzles) HEIGHT Maximum 30m SIMILAR SPECIES None.

JAN	FEB	MAR	APR	MAY	JUN	JUL	AUG	SEP	OCT	NOV	DEC

YEW

Taxus baccata

The Yew is a tree of life and death, living to an almost unimaginable age (2,000 years or more), and a symbol of permanence, but at the same time bearing toxic chemicals that are a threat to livestock and people alike. The only non-toxic parts are the fleshy fruits, which are gorged on by birds in late summer and autumn; the birds consume the flesh but discard the lethally poisonous seeds. The Yew has dense foliage and the rare Yew forests of southern England are mysterious, dark, astonishing places. The foliage is ideal for thick hedges and topiary. The Yew grows as a shrub or broad, rounded tree with an extraordinary thick trunk.

Woods, especially on chalk. Planted in cemeteries, parks and gardens. Common, but much scarcer towards the north.

ABOVE RIGHT: *TRUNK ALMOST PURPLE*

BELOW RIGHT: *LEAVES IN NEAT, FLAT ROWS*

dense, dark foliage

FACT FILE

FAMILY Taxaceae (Yews) HEIGHT Maximum 28m SIMILAR SPECIES Distinctive, but cypresses may have similar shapes (leaves feathery).

Easily identified by heavy cloak of evergreen leaves and, in autumn, by the fleshy fruits that are unique in a conifer. **LEAVES** Needles, soft to the touch, glossy green, and arranged in two rows, one on either side of the twig, in a relatively flat plane. They grow to 4cm long and 3mm wide, with a distinct point at the end. **FLOWERS** Female flowers green and bud-like, and just 1.5cm long. Male flowers yellow bud-like structures that look to have grown overly long, unruly hair. **FRUITS** Completely different from anything produced by any other conifer, so female Yews are unmistakable in summer and autumn. Fruit is a red, fleshy cup (known as an aril), inside which you can see the seed (when developing, the arils look like acorns). Each aril is 1cm in diameter. **BARK** Distinctly reddish-brown and may flake to reveal even deeper, almost purple colour.

Male and female flowers are on separate trees. **SEED** Single, inside fleshy aril, dispersed by birds. Male flowers release pollen into the wind. **LONGEVITY** 2,000+ years; one of the longest-lived trees in Europe.

Fighting men throughout the ages have been killed by weapons made of Yew, famously crossbows. Yew foliage is also perfect for topiary.

Often all but eliminated from farming areas since it is so toxic to livestock – hence its abundance in churchyards.

ABOVE LEFT: *MALE FLOWERS*

ABOVE RIGHT: *OLIVE-LIKE, FLESHY FRUITS*

BELOW: *DEVELOPING FRUITS*

Planted abundantly in parks and gardens.

JAN	FEB	MAR	APR	MAY	JUN	JUL	AUG	SEP	OCT	NOV	DEC

LAWSON'S CYPRESS

Chamaecyparis lawsoniana

Cypresses are renowned for their feathery and often scented leaves, which grow so dense that the trunk may be completely screened. The foliage is nothing like the usual 'needles' displayed by most conifers. In fact, the leaves are just 'scales' cloaking the shoots like a sheaf, arranged in fours, one for each 90 degrees. They look as though they slot together, like some plastic kit for crafts. Overall, the foliage resembles blue-green skeletal fingers, soft to the touch.

feathery foliage, obvious even at a distance

This is a large (42m or more tall), well-clothed evergreen tree with a cone-like shape and drooping top to the crown. Cypresses have very distinctive leaves and female cones. The bark is also worth checking. **LEAVES** Finger-like, feathery shoots/leaves easy to recognize and just 2mm

reddish-brown with neat, vertical ridges

FACT FILE

FAMILY Cupressaceae (Cypresses & Junipers) HEIGHT Maximum 65m SIMILAR SPECIES
There are many similar cypresses. The Giant Sequoia (p. 22) has similar foliage.

long. They give off a scent of parsley. Foliage is flattened and all in one plane. The shoots often droop. **CONES** Female cones unique. They begin small and bluish, developing into pea-like structures with 6–10 large scales, 8mm across. They are globular and look a bit like frozen peas. Male pollen cones in March bud-like and red (turning brown), like painful fingertips. **BARK** Red-brown with smart vertical ridges. The main trunk often forks.

ABOVE LEFT: LEAVES SLOT TOGETHER ON FEATHERY STEMS

ABOVE RIGHT: PEA-LIKE CONES

 Individual trees bear male and female parts. Pollen released from male cones drifts on the wind to female cones, which then close and mature. They mature in one year. **SEEDS** Released from female cones at any time of year. **LONGEVITY** Up to 600 years.

 You could be shot by an arrow made from Lawson's Cypress wood, and be buried in a coffin made from the same wood.

 In common with most conifers, female cones produce 'pollination drops' at the end of each scale. They are sticky and trap wind-borne pollen. The drop then dries and the pollen is pulled down towards the seeds.

LEYLAND CYPRESS
Cupressus x *leylandii*
This is the tree everybody loves to hate, a staple in suburbia to delineate boundaries, unremittingly dense and shading, and often causing neighbourhood rifts. Garden birds are more enthusiastic about it, using its branches for roosting, nesting and as a song post. It can grow 2m in a single year. The tree can be identified by its dense foliage, which on close examination is in three dimensions. It rarely produces cones.

ITALIAN CYPRESS
Cupressus sempervirens
The shapely icon of the Mediterranean countryside, this species is dense and column-like, with 3D foliage sprays and grey-brown bark.

JAN	FEB	MAR	APR	MAY	JUN	JUL	AUG	SEP	OCT	NOV	DEC

COMMON JUNIPER

Juniperus communis

The species is found in old pine woodland, rocky areas on open moorland, and chalk lowland. It is native.

Loved by gin aficionados everywhere, the Common Juniper is an unassuming little conifer, seen usually as a low-spreading, cloudy bush. For much of the year it looks rather like many other conifers, but those dark juicy berries – which can take up to an astonishing three years to ripen – are a giveaway in mid–late summer. It is one of only three conifers native to Britain (along with the Scots Pine, p. 34, and Yew, p. 16) and is very slow growing, surviving for up to 200 years in favourable conditions.

It is difficult to identify it by shape alone, as its growth is influenced by its surroundings. **LEAVES** Needles arranged in whorls of three along a woody stem. Each needle measures up to 1cm long, and has one white band along the length of the underside. **CONES** Male cones small, knobbly and yellow, growing in clusters; mature March–April. **FRUITS** Female trees can be found with ripe or unripe 'berries' most of the year. The mature female cones – single berries arranged along the stem, start out green and ripen to matte slate-blue/purple; approximately 7mm in diameter in around three

prickly-looking dense foliage

often looks ragged

years. **BARK** Greyish-brown, smooth when young, and becoming increasingly peeled and fibrous vertically with age.

 This species is dioecious, with male and female cones growing on separate trees. Fertilization happens by wind pollination. **SEEDS** Arranged in threes on each female cone. **LONGEVITY** Up to 200 years.

 The berries are used as the main flavouring in gin.

 Junipers, with their prickly, protective canopy, are ideal shelter for small birds such as the Goldcrest and Firecrest.

BELOW: *LADEN WITH RIPE 'BERRIES'*

FACT FILE

FAMILY Cupressaceae (Cypresses & Junipers) HEIGHT Maximum 8m SIMILAR SPECIES Other juniper species; other short-needled conifers.

JAN	FEB	MAR	APR	MAY	JUN	JUL	AUG	SEP	OCT	NOV	DEC

GIANT SEQUOIA

Sequoiadendron giganticum

Planted widely in parks. Introduced from California.

This is a massive evergreen tree with a huge trunk, growing to 57m in Europe. It is no less than the largest tree in the world, towering over the landscape, and is instantly recognizable. The trunk often looks too large for the branches and foliage, and it is distinctively heavily ridged at the base, and strongly tapering.

BELOW: *FEATHERY FOLIAGE USUALLY WELL CLEAR OF THE GROUND*

This species can be identified by its trunk and leaves, while the reproductive parts can be hard to see. **TRUNK** Massive and broad, with spongy bark that is resistant to fire. It is ridged, like a chocolate flake. **LEAVES** These are often out of reach for identification. Dense and dark, and feathery, similar to the leaves of a cypress, and 6–12mm long.

ABOVE: *UNIQUE, SPONGY, FIREPROOF BARK*

FACT FILE

FAMILY Cupressaceae (Cypresses & Junipers) HEIGHT Maximum 95m SIMILAR SPECIES
Two other species are also called redwoods – the Coast Redwood *Sequoia sempervirens* and
Dawn Redwood *Metasequoia glyptostroboides*. Also known as the Wellingtonia.

BELOW: *ROUND AND QUITE SMALL CONES*

imperiously tall →

CONES Female cones brown, with scales arranged in spirals. They are 4–7cm long, and a single tree may bear 11,000 cones.

 Individual trees bear male and female parts. Pollen released from male cones drifts on the wind to female cones, which then close and mature. **SEEDS** Emerge from female cones and are 4–5mm long, winged, and may fall 180m from the tree. Pollen cones are small, like a tiny bishop's mace. **LONGEVITY** Known to reach 3,200 years.

 Mainly an ornamental tree.

 In some parts of California, you can drive a car under a tunnel carved into a Giant Sequoia's trunk.

 The bark can be a metre thick.

JAN	FEB	MAR	APR	MAY	JUN	JUL	AUG	SEP	OCT	NOV	DEC

Found in parks and large estates. Introduced from the Middle East. Fairly common.

CEDAR OF LEBANON

Cedrus libani

Cedars are magnificent trees whose great, level storeys of foliage look like steps for giants to climb up them. Their stately, regal appearance has long been deemed ideal to show off the equally stately homes of the powerful and influential, and they have been planted in Europe since the 1740s. The Cedar of Lebanon originates from the eastern Mediterranean. Many of the original forests, including those in Lebanon, have been cut down.

Easily identified by its shape, leaves and cones. **SHAPE** Enormous broad trunk, often with huge lower branches. Also broad and spreading. The side branches towards the top are notably horizontal. **LEAVES** Needles to 3cm long, arranged in spirals on long

great plates of foliage

shoots, or in clusters of 10–60 on short side shoots. The latter give the appearance of tinsel. **CONES** Male (pollen) cones produced singly on a shoot. They are erect, starting greyish and becoming tired brown, slightly resembling an eaten corn-on-the-cob. Female cones easy to recognize, erect, in clusters and with a distinctive beer-barrel shape. They look papery, a little like exotic wasps' nests. Male cones to 4–5cm long; female cones 8–12cm long and 3–6cm wide. Male and female cones in autumn (September). **BARK** Decidedly greyish-black with dense scaling.

ABOVE LEFT: *SHOOTS LIKE TINSEL*

ABOVE RIGHT: *'BEER BARREL' FEMALE CONES*

BELOW: *BARK WITH DENSE SCALING*

Individual trees bear male and female parts. Pollen released from male cones drifts on the wind to female cones, which then close and mature. **SEEDS** Borne on the scales, and have small wings for dispersal. **LONGEVITY** Can live for 600 years or more.

The bark can be used as an insect repellent to protect clothes in drawers and cupboards.

Cedars sometimes drop quite large branches without warning, especially on warm summer days. This is a type of deliberate moulting.

FACT FILE

FAMILY Pinaceae (Pines) HEIGHT Maximum 42m SIMILAR SPECIES There are two other cedar species, the Deodar *C. deodara* and Atlas Cedar *C. atlantica*.

JAN	FEB	MAR	APR	MAY	JUN	JUL	AUG	SEP	OCT	NOV	DEC

EUROPEAN SILVER FIR

Abies alba

Native to mountains of Central Europe, including southern Poland and Germany, but widely planted as far north as southern Scandinavia; also occurs in the UK.

Silver Firs would be hard to distinguish from other conifers if it were not for their female cones that, unusually, stand upright on the stems. They are, however, usually high up. Otherwise, the Silver Fir is yet another conifer that, in the region, is mainly planted for forestry and recreational purposes. The latter includes its role in much of Europe as the original and current Christmas tree, dating from the sixteenth century. These days the Norway Spruce (p. 30) and (especially) the Caucasian (Nordmann) Fir *A. nordmanniana*, which are easier to grow, outdo the Silver Fir as the commercial leaders.

 Best identified by the female cones, but also note the leaves, bark, twigs and winter buds. **LEAVES** 2–3cm long, simple needles with a notch at the rounded end. They are arranged in two rows, one on either side of the twig, and crowded together. Each needle has silvery stripes. When they fall, they leave a disc-like scar. **BARK** Very grey and scaly. **TWIGS** Hairy. **CONES** Female cones stand upright on the branches (this is typical of most firs, larches and cedars, but not of other conifers planted in the region). They have the shape – to be

BELOW LEFT: *DISTINCTLY GREY BARK*

BELOW RIGHT: *MALE CONES*

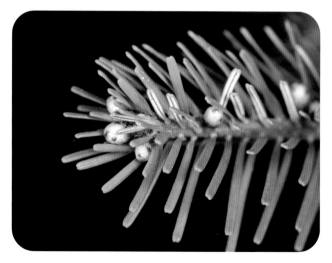

FACT FILE

FAMILY Pinaceae (Pines) HEIGHT Maximum 60m SIMILAR SPECIES Other firs (various planted species), Douglas Fir (p. 32) and other conifers.

honest – of a human poo. Male (pollen) cones small and high up. Female (seed) cones up to 20cm long, disintegrate on the tree. Small bracts project from the tightly packed, upwards pointing scales. **BUDS** Red-brown and blunt (see Douglas Fir).

Male and female reproductive parts are on the same tree. Pollen is blown in the wind. **SEEDS** Winged, with two attached to bracts on the cone. **LONGEVITY** 500–600 years.

Oil extracted from the tree can be extracted for use in perfumery.

Aphids on Silver Firs produce honeydew, much beloved by bees.

A seed can germinate under 1 per cent light.

tall with conical top

ABOVE: *CONES UPRIGHT ON STEM*

JAN	FEB	MAR	APR	MAY	JUN	JUL	AUG	SEP	OCT	NOV	DEC

EUROPEAN LARCH

Larix decidua

Found naturally in the mountains of Central Europe, but widely planted everywhere, including commercially.

Hands up those who thought that all conifers were evergreen. Many people are surprised to hear that needle-bearing trees may lose their leaves in autumn – but that is what the European Larch does, making it the only deciduous conifer in Europe. What is more, the needles turn a gorgeous gold in autumn, giving them a unique appearance, and going well with their shapely, often slightly drooping branches. Another distinction of this wonderful tree is the startling pink of the young female cones, quite a sight in the early spring.

Medium-sized to tall deciduous conifer, usually to 35m in height. It has horizontal branches. A very easy tree to identify, with its remarkable leaves and female cones. Take note of the shoots and bark, too. **LEAVES** The colours are radiant: a glorious

horizontal branches often curve upwards at the tip

BELOW: *AUTUMN COLOUR*

F A C T F I L E

FAMILY Pinaceae (Pines) HEIGHT Maximum 45m SIMILAR SPECIES Distinctive.

fresh green early in the year, then golden in autumn. Leaves produced in bunches, or tussocks, with up to 40 or so in each one. Leaves 3cm long, but less than 1mm wide. They mature in a year. **BARK** Greyish-brown and rough, with many fissures and ridges. **SHOOTS** In two lengths: long with few leaves, and short with lots of leaf-tussocks. They have a decidedly pink tinge. **CONES** Female cones, when young, are amazingly pink, often known as 'larch roses'. They make a wonderful contrast to the fresh green needles. When older they become brown and round, with shapely scales. They do not fall when ripe but may remain on the tree for several years. Male cones small, globular, like a soft toy's paws, and greenish-yellow. Male (pollen) cones yellowish, smaller than female cones. Female cones pink, 1cm across, and erect.

 Individual trees bear male and female parts. Pollen released from male cones drifts on the wind to female cones, which then close and mature. **SEEDS** Borne on cone scales, dispersed by the wind. **LONGEVITY** To 500 years, but usually about half that.

 A very popular tree for Bonsai cultivation.

 The Larch can tolerate temperatures of -50°C.

ABOVE LEFT: *FRESH SPRING FOLIAGE*

ABOVE CENTRE: *YOUNG FEMALE CONES IN SPRING*

ABOVE RIGHT: *OLDER FEMALE CONES*

BELOW: *GREYISH-BROWN BARK*

JAPANESE LARCH
Larix kaempferi
Widely grown in plantations. Differs by looking redder than the European Larch, has broader leaves and the cones have scales peeled back.

JAN	FEB	MAR	APR	MAY	JUN	JUL	AUG	SEP	OCT	NOV	DEC

NORWAY SPRUCE

Picea abies

Were it not for its status as the 'Christmas Tree' of homes, municipal squares and parks, the Norway Spruce would have few friends. It is dull, prickly, monotone and forms dense, funereally gloomy forests and plantations. It is a fast-growing tree with a satisfyingly pointed top.

In mountains in Europe and in the colder east and north. Planted for forestry and in parks. Not native to Britain.

 This evergreen tree can grow to 46m tall. It has distinctive leaves and stems. Look out also for the cones and bark. **LEAVES** Entirely dark green needles, each 1.5–3cm long with a spiky point, set on a small peg. When the leaves fall, the pegs remain, making the shoots prickly to the touch. The leaves are positioned in two rows, are four sided and tend to spread in all directions, making the foliage very dense. **BARK** Grey-brown, rough and prickly. It is not deeply fissured. **STEMS** Distinctively orange-brown. **CONES** Female (seed) cones are hanging, cylindrical and long, to 18cm, with neat, pointed scales. Male (pollen) cones small and yellowish.

ABOVE: *LARGE HANGING CONES*

BELOW: *ROUGH BARK WITHOUT DEEP FISSURES*

dark, dense foliage

 Male and female cones borne on the same tree. Wind pollinated. **SEEDS** Borne on scales of cones, which drop intact; released in spring. **LONGEVITY** To about 500 years.

 A hugely important forestry tree. You can make beer from it, as well as tea. The wood is used to make Stradivarius violins.

FACT FILE

FAMILY Pinaceae (Pines) HEIGHT Maximum 60m SIMILAR SPECIES Sitka Spruce (opposite) and other conifers.

JAN	FEB	MAR	APR	MAY	JUN	JUL	AUG	SEP	OCT	NOV	DEC

SITKA SPRUCE

Picea sitchensis

tall with conical top

purplish-grey bark

In Britain the Sitka Spruce accounts for almost half of all forestry plantations and is also common throughout the region in parks and gardens. It is fast growing and very salt tolerant.

Widely planted on all kinds of soil, including poor soils. Introduced from western North America; widespread.

 Tall evergreen tree with a broad conical top, usually to 50m in height. Best identified by the leaves, cones and shoots. **LEAVES** Unlike the Norway Spruce (opposite) – flattened in profile, bluer-green and more sharply pointed. They have two bluish stripes on the underside. They are also straight and set on woody pegs. Needles 3cm long. **SHOOTS** Whitish. **BARK** Purplish-grey, with the same rough papery texture as Norway Spruce's. **CONES** Female cones shorter than Norway Spruce's (to 10cm), but equally hang down and have triangular scales that fit tightly; however, they are slightly toothed. Whiten in autumn. Male cones oval, blunt and yellow.

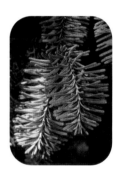

ABOVE: *DENSE NEEDLES IN FLAT PLANE*

BELOW: *FEMALE CONES IN AUTUMN*

Male and female cones grow on the same tree. Wind pollinated. **SEEDS** Tiny, winged and borne on the scales of cones, which drop intact. **LONGEVITY** To about 700 years.

A vastly important timber tree.

There is a single Sitka Spruce on Campbell Island in the sub-Antarctic. Planted 100 years ago, it is thought to be the most isolated tree in the world, 220km from the next nearest tree.

FACT FILE

FAMILY Pinaceae (Pines) HEIGHT Maximum 90m (USA) SIMILAR SPECIES Norway Spruce and other planted spruce species.

JAN	FEB	MAR	APR	MAY	JUN	JUL	AUG	SEP	OCT	NOV	DEC

DOUGLAS FIR

Pseudotsuga menziesii

This is one of the world's tallest trees, with a straight trunk and pointed top. Grows to 67m in Europe. It is shapely tree, with a straight trunk, slightly weeping branches and a somewhat half-dressed look. It is one of the world's tallest trees and accounts for many of Europe's loftiest tree specimens. It is also gorgeously aromatic, giving off a sweet scent of orange or other fruits, which is very obvious when you walk through plantations. It is shapely tree, with slightly weeping branches and a somewhat half-dressed look.

An important species in forestry plantations, also widely planted in parks and large gardens. Introduced from western North America.

 The tree is easiest to identify from its female cones, given a close look. Also check the leaves and winter buds. **LEAVES**

three-pointed bracts

needles radiate in all directions

FACT FILE

FAMILY Pinaceae (Pines) HEIGHT Maximum 100m SIMILAR SPECIES Other conifers, including spruces.

Very simple – 2 x 3cm-long, flat, unremarkable needles with two silvery stripes on the underside and blunt tips. They are very soft. Needles tend to radiate in all directions to envelop the twigs completely, so the foliage is very dense. **BARK** Grey-brown, corky and with deep vertical fissures. **BUDS** In winter narrow and pointed (blunt in the European Silver Fir, p. 26). **CONES** Female cones have unique three-pointed bracts on the scales that look as though there is a tongue sticking out at you, or as if some exotic bird has flown head-first into them. The cones hang down. Male (pollen) cones small, yellowish, oval and strongly clustered. Female (seed) cones up to 10cm long.

pointed top

slender, evergreen

 Male and female cones grow on the same tree. **SEEDS** Lie exposed on cone scales. **LONGEVITY** More than 1,000 years.

The timber is used for furniture and decking, among many other uses.

In the USA a rodent, the Red Tree Vole, lives its whole life in Douglas Fir canopies, often 30m up – but only the female does so. The male lives on the ground, so has a long climb in the breeding season to mate.

BELOW: *CORKY, GREY-BROWN BARK*

JAN	FEB	MAR	APR	MAY	JUN	JUL	AUG	SEP	OCT	NOV	DEC

SCOTS PINE

Pinus sylvestris

The Scots Pine is perhaps everyone's idea of what a conifer should look like, with its thick trunk and bushy bunches of dense, needle-like foliage. It is a tall evergreen tree, usually to 36m in height, with a rounded crown in mature trees. It is a native of northern Europe and often forms open forests. Scots Pine woods are excellent habitats for wildlife, including Red Squirrels.

Most common on sandy soils and acid heaths and moors, but very widely planted and grows on calcareous soils particularly in south of region. Native.

Easiest to recognize by bark, leaves and female cones. **LEAVES** The needles are in pairs on short side shoots, which are set spirally along the twigs. The bluish-green needles typically twist around, and are 2–8cm long. **BARK** Noticeably warm reddish-brown. On old trees, base is darker but upper branches still glow pinkish. The papery bark flakes. The long, bare, colourful trunk and lofty blobs of thick foliage are characteristic. **CONES** Female cones egg shaped, hanging solitarily. They are green for a year or so, then go brown, and are 2.5–7cm long. There is a raised bump at the top of each scale. Male (pollen) cones very small, borne in clusters at the bases of shoots, and yellow. Pollen is shed May–June.

Individual trees bear both male and female parts. Pollen released from male cones drifts on the wind to female cones, which then close and mature. **SEEDS** On cone scales, and dispersed by the wind. Male cones open in May. Pollen shed May–June. **LONGEVITY** To 700 years, but usually about 150 years.

Good for wildlife. Also for timber, and particularly used for telegraph poles.

thick trunk often reddish towards top

FACT FILE

FAMILY Pinaceae (Pines) HEIGHT Maximum 45m SIMILAR SPECIES Other pines, spruces and firs.

JAN	FEB	MAR	APR	MAY	JUN	JUL	AUG	SEP	OCT	NOV	DEC

AUSTRIAN PINE

Pinus nigra ssp. *nigra*

rugged, heavy-limbed

This is a rugged, tough pine from European mountains, where it can withstand temperatures down to -30°C. It is a heavy, broad-crowned evergreen tree that usually grows to 30m in height. It is frequently planted for shelterbelts and parks, thriving on almost any kind of soil, and often spreading under its own steam.

Planted widely, especially on sandy and light soils. Introduced from eastern Europe.

ABOVE: *DARK TRUNK*

BELOW: *TYPICAL PAIRED LEAF NEEDLES.*

 Best identified by trunk, branches, bark and leaves. **TRUNK** and **BRANCHES** Flatter top than in the Corsican Pine (p. 36), is not as tall and has many more branches. **BARK** A great deal rougher than that of the Corsican Pine, while being much darker than that of the Scots Pine (opposite). **LEAVES** Grow in pairs from small side shoots (as Corsican and Scots Pines), but are longer (8–12cm) than those of the Scots Pine, and shorter than the Corsican Pine's. They are noticeably darker than either. **CONES** Female cones cone shaped and up to 8cm long. Male (pollen) cones small and yellowish.

 Individual trees bear both male and female parts. Pollen released from male cones drifts on the wind to female cones, which then close and mature. **SEEDS** Borne on cone scales, and dispersed by the wind. **LONGEVITY** To 500 years.

 Often used for making paper.

FACT FILE

FAMILY Pinaceae (Pines) HEIGHT Maximum 50m SIMILAR SPECIES Corsican Pine, Scots Pine and other planted pine species. This species and the Corsican Pine may be lumped together under the name Black Pine.

JAN	FEB	MAR	APR	MAY	JUN	JUL	AUG	SEP	OCT	NOV	DEC

CORSICAN PINE

Pinus nigra ssp. *laricio*

This straight, tall evergreen tree with light foliage, is closely related to the Austrian Pine (p. 35) and is widely planted all over the region. It is a fast-growing tree that is a favourite for coastal shelterbelts, thriving on sandy soils.

Native to the Mediterranean and often planted on sandy and other dry soils.

 Best identified by trunk, branches, bark and leaves. **TRUNK** and **BRANCHES** Trunk long and bare, and crown relatively narrow with short side branches. Neater than the Austrian Pine. **BARK** Greyish, with narrow and broad dark vertical bands, and purple tinge. **LEAVES** Bright green and occur in pairs on side shoots (as Scots and Austrian Pines), but needles are much longer (up to 18cm). **CONES** Young 'flowers' whitish. Later on, cones are yellowish-brown, up to 8cm long. Male (pollen) cones small, yellowish and in clusters.

ABOVE: *GREYISH BARK WITH PURPLE TINGE*

BELOW: *FEMALE CONES*

 Individual trees bear both male and female parts. **SEEDS** Occur on cone scales, and are dispersed by the wind. **LONGEVITY** Up to 500 years in the Mediterranean.

 Used for plywood and building materials, but less durable than the Scots Pine (p. 34).

⭐ Can gain 60cm a year.

long, bare trunk

FACT FILE

FAMILY Pinaceae (Pines) **HEIGHT** Maximum 50m **SIMILAR SPECIES** Austrian Pine, Scots Pine and other pines not mentioned here.

JAN	FEB	MAR	APR	MAY	JUN	JUL	AUG	SEP	OCT	NOV	DEC

STONE PINE

Pinus pinea

umbrella-like shape

Mainly sandy soils in the Mediterranean. Planted in gardens and parks.

A distinctive conifer, with its broad, umbrella-like top, usually to 20m tall. It is instantly recognizable and is found widely in small gardens and parks towards the south of the region.

The branches are the most obvious feature. Check out the leaves and female cones, too. **BRANCHES** The many branches all spread out towards the top, giving the tree its unmistakable crown of dense needles. **TRUNK** Relatively short. **LEAVES** Occur in pairs from small side shoots. They diverge quite stiffly, and are up to 15cm long, sometimes more. **CONES** Female cones broad and round, 10cm across and glossy. Male (pollen) cones very small. **BARK** Flaky, with greyish and reddish parts.

ABOVE: *FLAKY, REDDISH BARK*

BELOW: *VERY LONG NEEDLES*

Individual trees bear both male and female parts. **SEEDS** Relatively enormous, 2cm long and bird dispersed. **LONGEVITY** 50–150 years.

Seeds are edible, a delicacy called 'pine nuts'.

 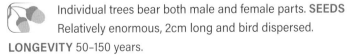

F A C T   F I L E

FAMILY Pinaceae (Pines) HEIGHT Maximum 25m SIMILAR SPECIES Distinctive.

JAN	FEB	MAR	APR	MAY	JUN	JUL	AUG	SEP	OCT	NOV	DEC

CRACK WILLOW

Salix x fragilis

At first glance, it does not seem like a great career move to be prone to damage, to crack under the weight of your own branches, or for your limbs to snap in the wind or succumb to snow. However, the Crack Willow is still a very common tree of riversides and marshes, albeit one that is often a right mess, broken and uneven. It is a spreading deciduous tree usually to 15m tall, which is abundantly pollarded.

Largely confined to watersides, especially rivers. The hybrid with White Willow (opposite), is actually more common.

 Recognized by twigs, leaves and bark. **TWIGS** Narrow and brittle, snapping loudly if bent; hairless and dark brown. **LEAVES** Narrow and long (9–15cm long, 1.5–3cm wide). They are shiny green above (like the White Willow's, opposite) but hairless below, so lack the stark whiteness. They are abundantly serrated. **BARK** Greyish and particularly heavily fissured, with a criss-crossing pattern. **FLOWERS** Catkins of both sexes slender, long and yellow; 4–6cm long. Spent female catkins (fruits) become downy. **BUDS** Tawny-brown, flat to the twig and have a single scale. Spirally arranged.

ABOVE: *NARROW LEAVES TYPICAL OF MANY WILLOWS*

BELOW: *BUDS FLAT TO THE TWIG*

 Male and female flowers on different plants. **SEEDS** Embedded in silky hairs; wind and water dispersed; need bare mud to germinate. **LONGEVITY**. Pollarded trees have lived to around 1,000 years.

narrow leaves distinctive even at a distance

F A C T   F I L E

FAMILY Salicaceae (Willows & Poplars) HEIGHT Maximum 29m SIMILAR SPECIES Other willows, but especially the White Willow.

JAN	FEB	MAR	APR	MAY	JUN	JUL	AUG	SEP	OCT	NOV	DEC

WHITE WILLOW

Salix alba

large for a willow

This is a stout, substantial deciduous tree to 33m tall – the largest of the willows. It often has a heavy trunk and leaning crown, and is frequently pollarded. This is very much a waterside tree that you will not find far from riverbanks, ponds and marshes. It has a broad, spreading crown packed with leaves that dance in the wind. This is a late-flowering willow, the catkins appearing in April.

Occurs mainly in marshes and by streams and ponds. Native and widespread.

ABOVE: *LEAVES HAIRY UNDERNEATH*

BELOW: *LEAVES LONG AND NARROW*

 Best identified by its leaves, as well as its overall size. Also note the twigs, catkins and bark. **LEAVES** Very long (5–10cm) and narrow, just 0.5–1.5cm wide. They are always silkily haired on the underside, and when young are hairy above as well. They have a greyish hue on both sides and have many barely visible tiny teeth. **BARK** Grey-brown with deep fissures, often with crossing pattern. **TWIGS** Do not break easily (see Crack Willow, opposite). **FLOWERS** Female catkins 3–4cm long and yellow. Spent female catkins become downy. Male catkins 4–5cm long. Appears with leaves, late April.

Male and female flowers are on different plants. Male catkins insect pollinated. **SEEDS** Embedded in silky hairs. Wind dispersed and need bare mud to germinate. **LONGEVITY** About 20 years.

FACT FILE

FAMILY Salicaceae (Willows & Poplars) HEIGHT Maximum 33m SIMILAR SPECIES Other willows, but especially the Crack Willow.

JAN	FEB	MAR	APR	MAY	JUN	JUL	AUG	SEP	OCT	NOV	DEC

Abundant, especially in parks. May occur in wilder places.

WEEPING WILLOW

Salix x *sepulchralis*

One of the most evocative of trees of the region, both in name and in shape, this is a common riverbank and garden introduction. Its common name arises from the idea of rain 'weeping' as it drips down from the hanging branches. The stems are astonishingly long and it is a great experience to stand under a mature tree and feel the enveloping of its branches, which may be 6m long and reach the ground.

The Weeping Willow, with its unmistakable 'weeping' appearance, grows to 22m in height. It is easily identified by its branches. The leaves and bark are also worth a look. **BRANCHES** Arch over like a frozen yellow fountain. They start green but

LEFT & BELOW: *THE TREE IN WINTER AND SUMMER*

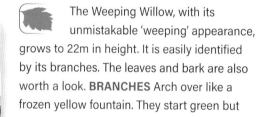

shape like a frozen fountain

then attain a golden colour. **LEAVES** Long and narrow. About 10 x 1cm, glossy-green above, pale but hairless below, and serrated. **BARK** Pale grey-brown (as most willows), with intertwining fissures. **FLOWERS** Catkins typically yellow, and hanging. About 8cm long and usually male.

ABOVE LEFT: LONG, DROOPING LEAVES

ABOVE RIGHT: MALE CATKINS

 Most plants are male clones of a hybrid and are infertile. **LONGEVITY** About 30 years.

 Very much an ornamental tree.

⭐ Weeping Willows are associated with mourning in many countries and are often grown in graveyards.

LEFT: BARK WITH INTERTWINING FURROWS; RIGHT: NARROW BUDS SET ALONG STEM

FACT FILE

FAMILY Salicaceae (Willows & Poplars) HEIGHT Maximum 22m SIMILAR SPECIES Other willows have long, narrow leaves. There are various types and hybrids of Weeping Willow.

JAN	FEB	MAR	APR	MAY	JUN	JUL	AUG	SEP	OCT	NOV	DEC

Various damp places.

BELOW: *NARROW LEAVES*

OSIER

Salix viminalis

The Osier must have been a godsend to ancient peoples, who soon recognized the extraordinary pliability of the fast-growing twigs. For centuries it has been used extensively for basket-weaving ('wickerwork') and still is today. There are many different hybrids and cultivated varieties, each with a different strength and pliability of twigs. The Osier is a distinctive deciduous shrub or small tree, usually to 6m tall. It is generally pollarded or coppiced.

Easiest to identify by its remarkable long leaves, but also has distinctive twigs. Additionally, check out the bark and flowers. **LEAVES** The narrowest of those of any willow, or indeed, any non-coniferous tree included in this book. They are at least six times as long as broad, but often much more, up to 15–25cm long and only 1cm broad. They grow at right angles to the stem and are silvery underneath. The edges are wavy, wrinkled and often roll inwards, as if drying out. **TWIGS** Exceptionally straight and long, like wands. They are yellowish and quickly lose any hairs. **FLOWERS** Male catkins (early spring) yellow, cylindrical and 2.5cm long. Female catkins greenish and up to 5cm long. **FRUITS** Spent female catkins become downy.

long, straight twigs

Male and female flowers are on different plants. **SEEDS** Embedded in silky hairs. Wind dispersed and need bare mud to germinate. Male catkins insect pollinated. **LONGEVITY** Typically 30 years.

Twigs incredibly pliable and perfect for basket-making.

FACT FILE

FAMILY Salicaceae (Willows & Poplars) HEIGHT Maximum 10m SIMILAR SPECIES Other willows, but especially the Crack Willow (p. 38) and White Willow (p. 39).

JAN	FEB	MAR	APR	MAY	JUN	JUL	AUG	SEP	OCT	NOV	DEC

GREY WILLOW

Salix cinerea

grey-brown bark

This is a very common species and its appearance is usually low and scrubby (to 6m) rather than as a well-developed tree. Along with the Goat Willow (p. 44), the Grey Willow produces early spring catkins known as 'pussy willows'.

Wet places of all kinds, including woods and marshes. Very common. Native.

ABOVE: *FEMALE CATKINS*

BELOW: *MALE CATKINS*

 Best identified by its leaves and twigs. Also check the flowers, buds and bark. **LEAVES** Much narrower and less plump than those of the Goat Willow (two or three times as long as broad, and 2–9cm long), and with less prominent veins. Greyish above. Underneath they may have rust-coloured hairs in summer (Britain and the west) or just be grey and downy (the east and Scandinavia). The margins often curl inwards. **TWIGS** Downy and very branched. If you peel back the bark, older (a year plus) twigs show ridges – but not in the Goat Willow. **BUDS** Small (3mm), hairy and red, lying prone to twigs. **FLOWERS** Male catkins 3cm long, narrower than those of the Goat Willow, but still bright yellow. Female catkins green and 5cm long. **BARK** Grey-brown, often with diamond-shaped markings.

 Male and female flowers grow on different plants. Male catkins insect pollinated. **FRUITS** Spent female catkins form capsules that release seeds. **SEEDS** Fluffy white, released in May and wind dispersed; need bare mud to germinate. **LONGEVITY** 30–40 years.

 Willow bark used to be chewed to relieve pain.

F A C T   F I L E

FAMILY Salicaceae (Willows & Poplars) HEIGHT Maximum 15m SIMILAR SPECIES All willows, but especially the Goat Willow. Often known as the Common Sallow.

JAN	FEB	MAR	APR	MAY	JUN	JUL	AUG	SEP	OCT	NOV	DEC

Damp ground, but will grow on rougher, drier ground and in open woodland.

ABOVE: 'PUSSY WILLOW' BLOSSOM

GOAT WILLOW

Salix capraea

Many people call it the 'pussy willow', due to the appearance of the male buds in early spring, which look furry like the paws of cats. The buds are a much-loved sign of coming spring, appearing well before the leaves in March, along with their bedfellows Common Hazel catkins (p. 68). This deciduous shrub or small tree, usually to 10m, is often domed and has one trunk with many branches.

No willows are easy to identify, but take note of the leaves, as well as the buds and flowers. **LEAVES** Rounder than those of other willows and 5–12cm long, with an overall oval shape – softly downy and silvery underneath, and when the wind blows the colour of the undersides may suddenly change the overall colour of the tree. They are less than twice as long as broad (see the Grey Willow, p. 43, and other willows). The veins are obvious. They hook slightly to the side at the tip. **BARK** Pale grey with shallow ridges. **BUDS** Unusual for having just one scale covering them. They are plump and reddish. **FLOWERS** Male catkins fluffy at first, then explode into yellow. Fairly round compared to those of other willows. Female catkins green, 3–7cm long. When releasing seeds, covered by woolly down.

Male and female flowers are on different plants. **SEEDS** Fluffy white, released in May and wind dispersed; need bare mud to germinate. **FRUITS** Spent female catkins release seeds. **FLOWERS** Insect pollinated. **LONGEVITY** To 300 years.

The wood is good for burning and for charcoal.

In contrast to other willows, does not grow from a cutting.

broader than most willows

FACT FILE

FAMILY Salicaceae (Willows & Poplars) HEIGHT Maximum 22m SIMILAR SPECIES All willows, but especially the Grey Willow. Also known as the Common Sallow.

JAN	FEB	MAR	APR	MAY	JUN	JUL	AUG	SEP	OCT	NOV	DEC

DWARF WILLOW

Salix herbacea

There are some mighty giant trees in this book but, just to show the astonishing variety of woody plants in the region, there is the Dwarf Willow, one of the smallest trees in the world. It can just about reach 10cm tall and forms a mat of creeping stems that might expand to 10–50cm, with each twig 2–3cm long. Its size is related to the extreme Arctic-Alpine environment in which it lives. It forms patches.

Found in rocky outcrops and on tundra, both on mountaintops and at low levels in the Arctic. Native and common.

 The tree's sheer small size and the creeping, patch-forming nature of the branches are unusual. The branches may even creep just underground. Each shoot may only have 2–3 leaves. **LEAVES** Very rounded, shiny green above, and with prominent veins and subtle teeth; 0.3–2.0cm long and broad. **FLOWERS** Tiny reddish catkins. Male catkins turn yellow after pollen ripens. Flowers to 0.5cm.

 Male and female parts occur on different plants. **SEEDS** Dispersed by the wind. **FRUITS** Form from reddish spent catkins. Insect pollinated. **LONGEVITY** Unknown.

 None.

 This tree is thought to be grazed by Reindeer.

barely reaches 10cm above the ground

FACT FILE

FAMILY Salicaceae (Willows & Poplars). HEIGHT Can be as little as 1cm. SIMILAR SPECIES There are several other very small willows in the region.

JAN	FEB	MAR	APR	MAY	JUN	JUL	AUG	SEP	OCT	NOV	DEC

WHITE POPLAR

Populus alba

The summit of poplar perfection, the White Poplar lives up to its name when a breeze blows, turning over the grey-green leaves to reveal their gleaming white undersides, caused by downy hairs beneath. The tree really does look startling white among other trees. In northern Europe it is an introduced ornamental tree, common on street corners and, especially, as a windbreak. This medium-sized, spreading deciduous tree always leans, and grows to 20m. It suckers strongly. It is tolerant of poor soils and salt spray, and manages to grow fast in either.

Planted by roadsides and in parks, and often in sand dunes and other coastal areas. Introduced from Europe.

Most easily identified by its leaves, bark, twigs and buds, although check the flowers, too. **LEAVES** Downy underneath, with downy stalks, and contrastingly green and shiny above. The shape of the leaves varies. They are basically five lobed, vaguely resembling a maple but on some trees the shoots may be rounder. Each leaf 4–15cm long. **BARK** Distinctively pale grey with lots of diamond-shaped black

ABOVE: *MALE CATKINS*

BELOW: *LEAVES DOWNY UNDERNEATH*

lobed leaves on long stalks

FACT FILE

FAMILY Salicaceae (Willows & Poplars) HEIGHT Maximum 20m SIMILAR SPECIES Other poplars, Aspen (p. 54) and willows.

leaves
whitish
underneath

gashes and neat vertical fissures. **TRUNK** Leans (typical of poplars). **TWIGS** Densely downy and whitish. **BUDS** Frostily downy, blunt and rusty-red. Arranged spirally and 4–5mm long. **FLOWERS** Catkins slender and yellow. Male catkins grey with red stamens, 4–8cm long; female catkins yellow, to 8–10cm long.

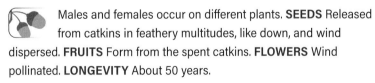

Males and females occur on different plants. **SEEDS** Released from catkins in feathery multitudes, like down, and wind dispersed. **FRUITS** Form from the spent catkins. **FLOWERS** Wind pollinated. **LONGEVITY** About 50 years.

Bark used to be ground down and used in a mixture to rub haemorrhoids.

Almost every cultivated tree in the region is female.

Poplar seeds, carried on their down, may be dispersed as much as 30km by the wind.

ABOVE & TOP LEFT: *THE TREE IN WINTER AND SUMMER*

BELOW: *BUDS FROSTILY DOWNY*

JAN	FEB	MAR	APR	MAY	JUN	JUL	AUG	SEP	OCT	NOV	DEC

Planted beside water, such as ponds and streams, and in damp woods.

GREY POPLAR

Populus x canescens

A hybrid between the Aspen (p. 54) and White Poplar (p. 46), this is a commonly planted, tall, spreading deciduous tree. It produces suckers and makes thickets, and is most like the White Poplar, certainly in its trunk and leaves, the latter being frosty, if not heavily downy beneath, making it look 'grey' rather than 'white'. It shows so-called 'hybrid vigour' and can shoot up to 40m, with large, heavy arching branches.

heavy limbs

 Most easily identified by the bark, leaves and flowers; the twigs and buds are also worth checking. **BARK** Similar to that of the White Poplar, greyish with distinctive black diamond-shaped pits. **LEAVES** Vary and are confusing, some being Aspen-like and round, others more like maple leaves, with spiky lobes. On suckers they are woolly below. Leaves to 10cm long. **FLOWERS** Reddish catkins, a little bit woolly (like those of the Aspen but not Black Poplar, opposite). Male catkins 5cm long and hanging; female catkins rare. **TWIGS** Soon become hairless. **BUDS** Woolly at base, 6–10mm long, with whitish tips.

BELOW: *MALE CATKINS*

 Males and females occur on different plants. **SEEDS** Released from catkins in feathery multitudes, like down. Wind dispersed. **FRUITS** Form from the spent catkins. **FLOWERS** Wind pollinated. **LONGEVITY** 50 years or more.

FACT FILE

FAMILY Salicaceae (Willows & Poplars) HEIGHT Maximum 46m SIMILAR SPECIES Other poplars; willows.

JAN	FEB	MAR	APR	MAY	JUN	JUL	AUG	SEP	OCT	NOV	DEC

BLACK POPLAR

Populus nigra

There is nothing quite like the presence of a mature Black Poplar, especially in early spring, with its huge, airy top, its bark tinged orange and its red catkins aglow. It is a majestic, characterful tree, with a craggy trunk, huge, spreading branches and a habit of always leaning one way or another. Very much a waterside tree, now rare in Britain, it is still common on the Continent. Its branches arch downwards, and it does not produce suckers.

Usually occurs by streams, rivers and ponds, especially in floodplains.

 Most easily identified by the leaves, trunk and flowers; also check the bark, twigs and buds. **LEAVES** Classic Ace of Spades shape, and minutely toothed (see Aspen, p. 54). Smaller than leaves of other poplars (except the Aspen); just 7cm long. **TRUNK** Dark with knobbly bosses at the base. **BARK** Dark grey, with irregular vertical fissures. Often looks black, hence the name. **FLOWERS** Male catkins have a reddish tinge from the anthers. Female catkins greenish, woolly in spring (May), with white hairs. Both to 5cm long. **TWIGS** Hairless, knobbly and golden-brown. **BUDS** Orange-brown, hairless and sticky; 7–10mm long.

ABOVE: *CLASSIC 'ACE OF SPADES' LEAF SHAPE*

 Males and females occur on different plants. **SEEDS** released from catkins in feathery multitudes; wind dispersed. Drop in May. **FRUITS** Form from spent catkins. **FLOWERS** Wind pollinated. **LONGEVITY** Up to 200 years.

 Once used to make cart wheels and also floorboards.

airy canopy

FACT FILE

FAMILY Salicaceae (Willows & Poplars) HEIGHT Maximum 40m SIMILAR SPECIES Grey Poplar (opposite), Aspen, hybrids and willows.

JAN	FEB	MAR	APR	MAY	JUN	JUL	AUG	SEP	OCT	NOV	DEC

HYBRID BLACK POPLAR

Populus x canadensis

Usually planted in wet areas, for example beside ponds and rivers, often in parks. Used as shelter.

In many places in the region, especially the UK, Hybrid Black Poplars are the most common poplars of all. They are a cross between the Black Poplar (p. 49) and American Cottonwood *P. deltoides*, which arose in France in the eighteenth century, and are frequently planted as amenity trees. They make their mark. In April the beautiful red catkins quickly fall and may litter the ground below. Almost all hybrids are males, but females of some cultivars occur, and they litter the ground with their down later in the season.

Similar to the Black Poplar, but look for details in the trunk, branches and leaves. The flowers are usually obvious. Also check the bark and buds. **TRUNK** Straighter than the Black Poplar's and the tree is often taller. It is usually tidy, lacking the bosses and burrs typical of the Black Poplar. **BRANCHES** Erect, pointing upwards and not arching over, as in the Black Poplar. **LEAVES** Similar to those of the Black Poplar, but have 1–2 small red glands at the bases of the leaf stalks; 8cm long. **FLOWERS** Short, plump, bright crimson catkins, like little sausages. Most planted Hybrid Black Poplars are males. Female flowers are yellow-green catkins. They turn woolly in summer and

BELOW LEFT: *RED GLANDS AT BASE OF LEAF STALKS*

BELOW RIGHT: *LEAVES HAVE LONG STALKS*

ABOVE: *BARK SMOOTHER AND GREYER THAN BLACK POPLAR*

Tall, usually straight deciduous tree without suckers, generally to 40m in height.

may litter the ground with their down in July. **BARK** usually greyer than the Black Poplar's, and not as irregularly craggy. **BUDS** Long and sticky.

 Males and females are on different plants. **SEEDS** Released from catkins in feathery multitudes, like down, and wind dispersed. Drop in June/July. **FRUITS** Form from spent catkins. **FLOWERS** Wind pollinated. **LONGEVITY** 40–60 years or more.

 You might be holding this book with an artificial limb made from Hybrid Black Poplar wood.

The size of the largest leaf on a branch is an indication of how much wood a Hybrid Black Poplar will grow in a given year.

FACT FILE

FAMILY Salicaceae (Willows & Poplars) HEIGHT Maximum 40m SIMILAR SPECIES Other poplars.

JAN	FEB	MAR	APR	MAY	JUN	JUL	AUG	SEP	OCT	NOV	DEC

Cultivated hybrid, abundant.

LOMBARDY POPLAR

Populus nigra var. *italica*

Although it is one of the most recognizable of all deciduous trees in the European landscape, especially in warmer areas, the Lombardy Poplar is not found in the wild anywhere. It is a cultivated variety of the Black Poplar (p. 49), famous for its narrow shape, in which the branches grow up almost vertically, making the tree as narrow as a pillar. It lives fast

classic columnar shape

FACT FILE

FAMILY Salicaceae (Willows & Poplars) HEIGHT Maximum 36m SIMILAR SPECIES Other poplars and the Aspen (p. 54).

and loose, growing very rapidly for 15 years or so, then burning out, dying of infection or blowing over.

ABOVE: *LONG-STALKED TRIANGLES, TYPICAL OF POPLAR*

 The overall shape of the tree is key, especially the branches. Also look at the leaves, flowers and bark. **BRANCHES** Grow up at a steep angle, hugging close to the trunk to produce the very familiar vertical shape. Shoots often arise at the base (epicormic shoots). **LEAVES** Typical poplar-type leaves – long-stalked triangles. Densely packed. **FLOWERS** Reddish catkins about 12cm long, which are dense but not fluffy. Appear in spring before leaves. **BARK** Greyish-brown and decidedly craggy, looking old before its time.

BELOW: *GREYISH, CRAGGY BARK*

 Most trees are male; females (different trees) are rare. **SEEDS** (Rare) in woolly masses. **LONGEVITY** Rarely reaches 50 years; usually much less.

 Utilized everywhere as an attractive shelterbelt or boundary.

 The tree can grow 2m a year.

JAN	FEB	MAR	APR	MAY	JUN	JUL	AUG	SEP	OCT	NOV	DEC

ASPEN

Populus tremula

Grows in any type of soil, in woods, heaths, moors and uplands, and sometimes in damp areas. Native, common and northern.

This is probably the only tree that you could identify by the sound that it makes. In summer, it takes the merest breeze to stir the leaves into a soothing symphony of gentle whispering, sounding like light rain or a babbling brook – a marvel for relaxation. The leaves quiver easily because they are set on long, slender, flattened stalks. The Aspen is a slender tree that grows to about 20m tall, with an airy crown. It forms thickets of suckers. It is common but overlooked, easily colonizing bare ground and preferring open sunlight.

 Tricky. Look out for the distinctive leaves, bark and winter buds. It forms catkins in spring. **LEAVES** Unique in shape, very rounded but with neatly, artistically scalloped edges. Pale green. Long, thin stalks. Leaves slightly broader

bark looks silver from a distance

ABOVE: *BUDS STICKY AND SHARP-TIPPED*

than long. They are 2–8cm wide and long, and the leaf stalk is 4–8cm long. Autumn leaves turn golden-yellow in north (may just fall quickly in south). **BARK** Pale creamy-grey and might easily resemble the bark of a birch (pp. 60–62) from a distance. Quite smooth with horizontal rings of small, diamond-shaped markings. **BUDS** Sticky, sharp tipped, and closely set to the twig, pointing the same way; 7mm long. **FLOWERS** Male catkins 5–10cm long, purplish, deeply cut as if about to disintegrate, and fluffy. Female catkins similar but shorter (2–6cm), and green tinged pink.

ABOVE LEFT: CREAMY BARK WITH DARK RINGS

ABOVE RIGHT: DISTINCTIVE LEAVES WITH SCALLOPED EDGES

 Male and female occur on different trees. **SEEDS** dispersed by the wind. Male catkins produce pollen that is wind blown. Female catkins release minute, fluffy seeds that are also wind blown. **LONGEVITY** Short lived; rarely more than 50 years.

BELOW: FRAGILE-LOOKING MALE CATKINS

 Wood is not dangerously flammable, making it ideal for paper and for matches.

Whole 'woodlands' or thickets of Aspen can all effectively be a single plant, each separate tree forming from a sucker.

FACT FILE

FAMILY Salicaceae (Willows & Poplars) HEIGHT 15–25m SIMILAR SPECIES Other poplar species and also birches, which also have pale trunks.

JAN	FEB	MAR	APR	MAY	JUN	JUL	AUG	SEP	OCT	NOV	DEC

COMMON WALNUT

Juglans regia

Flourishes best in warm areas in full sun, on good soils. Introduced from southern Europe and planted widely.

Walnuts are one of the most recognizable and popular of all the edible nuts in the world, so it is hardly surprising that the tree is widely planted, even in the relative chill of northern Europe. It is a rather oak-like, spreading tree, one of the few in Europe with so-called pinnate leaves, in which the leaf is divided into leaflets equally on both sides of the stalk shaft, like a feather, with one leaflet at the end (hence an odd number of leaflets). This is a large, broadly spreading deciduous tree with a short trunk.

Easily recognized by its leaves, fruits and flowers. **LEAVES** Arranged in leaflets of 5–13, most frequently seven. They are 25–40cm long, including the leaflets, leathery, untoothed and aromatic – resembling shoe polish to some people. Turn golden in autumn. **BARK** Decidedly grey, with flakes and pockmarks. **FRUITS** Shiny green globes, like miniature apples, dotted with minute pale glands. Contain one seed each; 5cm in diameter. **FLOWERS** Yellow-green hanging catkins on male trees, 5–10cm long and wind pollinated. Females' flowers erect, and also yellow. Catkins appear before leaves.

BELOW LEFT: *LEAVES IN PAIRS WITH TERMINAL LEAF*

BELOW RIGHT: *THE FAMOUS FRUITS*

broad,
spreading
tree

Male and female parts grow on separate trees. **SEEDS**
Walnuts ripen in September, and are dispersed by animals.
LONGEVITY Reaches about 200 years.

Grown worldwide as a commercial foodstuff, but timber is
also highly valued.

The species may lose 90 per cent of its fine roots in a very
cold winter.

ABOVE LEFT: *FEMALE CATKINS*

ABOVE RIGHT: *GREYISH POCKMARKED BARK*

FACT FILE

FAMILY Juglandaceae (Walnuts) HEIGHT Maximum 35m SIMILAR SPECIES Any tree with
pinnate leaves, such as the Common Ash (p. 146).

JAN	FEB	MAR	APR	MAY	JUN	JUL	AUG	SEP	OCT	NOV	DEC

BOG MYRTLE

Myrica gale

Mainly found on acid soils in bogs, moors and damp woodland. Native and locally common.

You could easily visit a moorland or heathland area and have no idea there was such a thing as Bog Myrtle, were it not for the scent given off by this aromatic shrub. Where it grows abundantly, the hot, balsam-like smell is all-pervasive, especially on a warm day when the shrub is in flower. Its oils have been used to scent candles, among many other things. The Bog Myrtle is a deciduous shrub up to 2.5m tall. It is often multi-trunked and suckers freely.

 Apart from the scent, most easily identified by the flowers (both male and female). Also check the leaves and twigs.

FLOWERS Catkins, which are rather small (1–2cm long). Male catkins orange and female catkins redder. Female catkins turn yellow in late

thick and low growing

F A C T   F I L E

FAMILY Myricaceae (Bog Myrtles) HEIGHT Maximum 2.5m SIMILAR SPECIES None. Also known as the Sweet Gale.

summer as the fruits develop. Flowers before leaves. **LEAVES** Greyish-green and rather narrow, especially at the base, but rounded at tip. Turn yellow in October. Downy. They are covered with glands, appearing as small yellow dots, and are 2–6cm long. They are slightly toothed. **TWIGS** Distinctive reddish-brown and, like the leaves, have scent-producing glands.

ABOVE LEFT: BUDS

ABOVE RIGHT: NARROW LEAVES ROUNDED AT TIP

 Male and female flowers usually on different plants, but not always; some plants are hermaphrodite. **SEEDS** Dispersed by water. **FRUITS** Nuts with wings. **LONGEVITY** About 30 years.

 The extracted oil is sometimes used as an ingredient in midge repellent, with apparently impressive results.

 The species can colonize poor soils because its root nodules house a bacterium (*Frankia*) that fixes nitrogen (as Alder, p. 64).

BELOW LEFT & RIGHT: FEMALE CATKINS TURN YELLOW

| JAN | FEB | MAR | APR | MAY | JUN | JUL | AUG | SEP | OCT | NOV | DEC |

SILVER BIRCH

Betula pendula

Grows on light, acid soils, in woods, scrub, heaths and moors, on marginal land. Forms its own woods. Also widely planted.

There can be few easier trees to identify than the slender, graceful Silver Birch, with its unmistakable, paper-like white bark. It is thought that the white bark protects the tree from ultraviolet rays from the sun during the endless Arctic days in summer. Birch seeds are winged like miniature bats and are dispersed as easily as dust, soon settling just about anywhere. They often produce the first trees to colonize new ground, for example after a fire. The canopy of the Silver Birch is light and airy, and birch woods are fantastic places for many forms of wildlife. This is a medium-sized, straight-trunked tree, usually to 25m tall. Typically, it has descending branches (some 'weeping').

 Easily identified by its bark (but see Downy Birch, p. 62). Also the leaves, catkins and buds. **BARK** Famously white. Lower trunk often encrusted with black diamond-shaped gashes, while the base can be crusty and black. **LEAVES** Shaped like the Ace of Spades, triangular and hairless (see also Downy Birch), and 3–7cm long. They are also toothed. (Compare with limes, elms and the Crab Apple, p. 98). **FLOWERS** Male catkins (3–6mm long) form in the autumn and stay on the tree all winter; dormant until April/May. They are often in twos at the ends of twigs and hang down. Female catkins green and erect at first, then hang down. **BUDS** Small, pointed and shiny. **TWIGS** Hairless

BELOW LEFT: *'ACE OF SPADES' SHAPED LEAVES*

BELOW CENTRE: *MALE CATKINS, OFTEN IN PAIRS*

BELOW RIGHT: *FEMALE CATKIN*

ABOVE: *WHITE BARK WITH DEEP GASHES*

BELOW & RIGHT: *THE TREE IN WINTER AND SUMMER*

ends of branches droop

and have white warts (see also Downy Birch).

 Each individual tree bears male and female flowers. **SEEDS** Minute (1–2mm long) and winged, as if wearing a wingsuit for base jumping. They are wind dispersed. **FRUITS** These are the old female catkins; they disintegrate on the tree to be dispersed. **FLOWERS** Male catkins wind pollinated. **LONGEVITY** Usually no more than 50 years.

 Good as firewood and plywood, and twigs are ideal for broomsticks. Wine can be made from it.

 In Scotland, birch seeds have been found on the ground in densities of 43,000 per metre.

BELOW: *SMALL, POINTED BUDS*

FACT FILE

FAMILY Betulaceae (Birches & Hazels) HEIGHT Maximum 31m SIMILAR SPECIES Downy Birch, and possibly Aspen (p. 54). There are other widely planted birch species.

| JAN | FEB | MAR | APR | MAY | JUN | JUL | AUG | SEP | OCT | NOV | DEC |

DOWNY BIRCH

Betula pubescens

This species is much less known than the Silver Birch (p. 60), but is still common. It is found in damper places and more often in northern, rugged areas. It has the distinction of growing further north than any other broadleaved tree. Its branches do not hang down like those of the Silver Birch and it has a denser crown.

Similar to that of the Silver Birch, but grows on wetter soils and on higher ground. Native. Most common towards the north, and widely planted.

 Easily identified by its bark (but see Silver Birch). The leaves and twigs also help distinguish it. **BARK** Famously white, but sometimes grey or even brown. It is also smoother than the Silver Birch's bark, without the contrasting black vertical diamonds or black crustiness at the base. It may have more horizontal grooves. **LEAVES** More rounded than those of the Silver Birch, especially at the base – somewhat egg shaped and shorter (2–5cm long). They are more neatly serrated, and have hairs on the stalks (not on the Silver Birch) and underneath. **FLOWERS** Male catkins 3–6cm long. **TWIGS** Softly hairy and smooth, without white warts.

 Each individual tree bears male and female flowers. **SEEDS** Each 1–2mm long and have smaller wings than those of the Silver Birch; they are wind dispersed. **FRUITS** These are the old female catkins; they disintegrate on the tree. **FLOWERS** Male catkins; wind pollinated. **LONGEVITY** Usually no more than 50 years.

 Outer layer of bark can be used for canoes.

 Each male catkin produces about 5.5 million pollen grains.

bark smoother than Silver Birch →

FACT FILE

FAMILY Betulaceae (Birches & Hazels) HEIGHT Maximum 27m
SIMILAR SPECIES Silver Birch.

JAN	FEB	MAR	APR	MAY	JUN	JUL	AUG	SEP	OCT	NOV	DEC

GREY ALDER

Alnus incana

broad crown

Although it is frequently found along rivers and lakes in the same way as its close relative, the Common Alder (p. 64), the Grey Alder also occurs in drier habitats away from moist soil. A native of continental Europe, it is found much further north than the Common Alder, right into the Arctic Circle. The name is appropriate, as both the trunk and the undersides of the leaves are distinctly grey. A small to medium-sized tree with a broad crown, the Grey Alder often suckers.

Often found in much drier places than the Common Alder, but also in wetlands. Native to continental Europe, and widely planted.

ABOVE: *CHARACTERISTIC GREY BARK*

BELOW: *BROAD LEAVES WITH SHARP TIP*

Most easily distinguished from the Common Alder by its bark and leaves. **BARK** Grey and often remarkably smooth, even in old individuals. The odd ominous crack does form, however. **LEAVES** Quite different in shape from those of the Common Alder, and also greyer green below, with hairs. They are pointed, with obvious teeth, and to 10cm long. Drops leaves when still green. **FLOWERS** Male catkins similar to those of the Common Alder, 2–6cm long; female catkins blob shaped, 1cm across. **FRUITS** Green female 'cones' rounder than those of the Common Alder. 1–1.8cm across.

Male and female flowers occur on the same tree. **SEEDS** Dispersed by the wind and water, falling from the fruits. Wind pollinated. **LONGEVITY** 60–100 years.

FACT FILE

FAMILY Betulaceae (Birches & Hazels) HEIGHT Maximum 23m
SIMILAR SPECIES Common Alder.

JAN	FEB	MAR	APR	MAY	JUN	JUL	AUG	SEP	OCT	NOV	DEC

COMMON ALDER

Alnus glutinosa

Damp woods, lakes and rivers.

Of all the trees in this book, this and the willows are the ones most closely associated with water. The Common Alder is an abundant riverside and lakeside tree, although it also occurs in damp patches in woodland. It is short-lived and quickly loses out to other trees if the soil becomes more fertile. This is one of the easiest trees to identify in winter, with its dense network of purplish twigs, spent fruits and, from February, catkins. It is a medium-sized deciduous tree, usually growing to 20m in height. It sometimes grows as a shrub.

Easily identified by the fact that it is always close to water.

BELOW & LEFT: *THE TREE IN WINTER AND SUMMER*

dense crown

FACT FILE

FAMILY Betulaceae (Birches & Hazels) HEIGHT Maximum 29m SIMILAR SPECIES Grey Alder (p. 63), birches (pp. 60–62). Leaves quite Hazel-like (p. 68).

The crown is dense with a purplish hue in winter – a very characteristic sight. Check out the catkins, leaves and fruits, as well as the buds and bark. **FLOWERS** Male catkins reddish through the winter and turn green in early spring, 2–6cm long. They hang in small clusters. Female flowers egg shaped, growing in small bunches like crinkled grapes, 1cm across. Green at first, then turning brown. **LEAVES** Rounded and blunt tipped – in fact, the tip is often characteristically indented. They are minutely toothed, with strongly defined veins, and 3–9cm long. **FRUITS** Just like small cones – the brush-like ends recall that of a honey dipper. **BUDS** Unusual for being mauve tinged, and club shaped or even like boxing gloves. **BARK** Dark purplish-brown and ruggedly crinkled, with vertical fissures.

TOP, LEFT TO RIGHT: *NOTCHED LEAVES, MALE CATKINS, FEMALE 'CONES'*

ABOVE: *RUGGED, CRINKLED BARK*

BELOW: *OLDER FEMALE 'CONES'*

 Male and female flowers found on the same tree. **SEEDS** Dispersed by the wind and water, falling from the fruits. **FRUITS** Look like cones, 1–3cm across. **FLOWERS** Wind pollinated. **LONGEVITY** Short-lived tree, lasting about 60 years.

 The wood does not rot in water, so has long been used for the deep foundations of buildings such as cathedrals.

 The Alder forms an association with a bacterium that grows on its roots and absorbs nitrogen from the air, transferring it to the tree, which can then grow in poor soil.

JAN	FEB	MAR	APR	MAY	JUN	JUL	AUG	SEP	OCT	NOV	DEC

HORNBEAM

Carpinus betulus

Common, especially on clay soils, where it can form its own woods, but usually not dominant. Also used in hedges. Native.

If you can 'overlook' a tree, the Hornbeam is a good candidate, a poor relation of the similar Common Beech (p. 70), and met with less often. It is not quite as tall or imposing as a Common Beech and does not form pure woodland so often. It does share an unusual habit with the beech, however – the dead leaves are often retained in winter on younger trees. The Hornbeam is often planted in parks and streets, and is found in hedges. The name 'Hornbeam' simply means 'hard tree', describing the famously tough wood, which is capable of blunting wood-turning instruments. This is a medium-sized, spreading deciduous tree, usually to 25m in height.

 You will spot the leaves first, but the fruits are unique. Also note the catkins, bark and buds. **LEAVES** Oval and pointed, with sharp-looking teeth along the edges – the teeth are of different sizes. The most obvious feature is the veins, which are so strongly pleated that they look as though they have been pressed in by a machine. There are 10–15 pairs of veins, and the leaf is shiny and rough. Each leaf is 3–11cm long. Beech leaves are not toothed, and have less obvious veins and elm leaves are not symmetrical. Turn yellow in autumn. **FRUITS** Nuts (1.2cm long), nestling in extraordinary, leafy, three-lobed bracts. These grow tightly together in bunches before falling, like ash keys (p. 146). **FLOWERS** Male flowers are drooping,

BELOW LEFT: *STRONGLY PLEATED LEAVES*

BELOW CENTRE: *GREYISH BARK*

BELOW RIGHT: *FRUIT BUNCHES*

BELOW & RIGHT: *THE TREE IN SPRING AND AUTUMN*

deep fissures →

knobbly catkins of the most delicate pale greenish, tinged reddish, 2.5–5cm long. Female flowers 3cm long, with bracts curling upwards. **BARK** Smooth and grey, with rather neat, wavy vertical fissures and pale streaks. **BUDS** Reddish, long and slender; they adhere close to the twigs and may appear to 'look around' them.

 Male and female flowers occur on the same tree. **SEEDS** Dispersed by the wind. **FLOWERS** Wind pollinated. **LONGEVITY** Up to 300 years.

 Wood, renowned for its toughness and hardness, once used for yoking ploughing oxen together, and for chopping blocks.

 The Hornbeam is the best tree for using a stethoscope to hear the rising spring sap moving, more forcefully than in any other tree.

BELOW: *MALE CATKINS*

F A C T   F I L E

FAMILY Betulaceae (Birches & Hazels) **HEIGHT** Maximum 32m **SIMILAR SPECIES** Common Beech. The Common Hazel (p. 68) has similar leaves.

JAN	FEB	MAR	APR	MAY	JUN	JUL	AUG	SEP	OCT	NOV	DEC

COMMON HAZEL

Corylus avellana

Woodland, hedgerows and scrub, on almost any soil type. Native and abundant.

The Common Hazel is, in every sense, an early arrival. Not only is it a hardy shrub that can be the first to colonize rough ground and which was quick to establish after the last ice ages, but it is also a living reminder of the inevitability of spring. Even in the middle of a cold, dark winter, it spouts forth its glorious lamb's tail catkins, each a small flag of resistance to the gloom. For centuries it has been of significance to people for its rich autumnal crop of nuts and extraordinary pliable wood, which can literally be bent and knotted. The Hazel is a shrub, generally to 6m tall and usually with multiple stems.

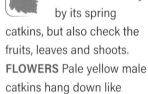

Easiest to identify by its spring catkins, but also check the fruits, leaves and shoots.

FLOWERS Pale yellow male catkins hang down like

RIGHT & BELOW: THE TREE IN WINTER AND SUMMER

multi-trunked habit is distinctive

FACT FILE

FAMILY Betulaceae (Birches & Hazels) HEIGHT Maximum 15m
SIMILAR SPECIES Common Alder (p. 64).

lamb's tails. Male catkins 2–8cm long. The peculiar female flowers, with their crimson styles, look like sea anemones. **FRUITS** Hazelnuts reside in tight-fitting, leafy husks that start green and turn brown. They are 2cm long. **LEAVES** Oval with pointed tips, and 5–12cm long. They are often tired looking, with a floppy feel, a rough texture and a covering of down. They have lots of small teeth. The stalk is also downy. **SHOOTS** Twigs covered with hairs. **BUDS** Plump, slightly hairy and plum-like.

 Male and female occur on separate flowers on the same plant. The tree does not self-pollinate. **SEEDS** Single nuts. **FLOWERS** Wind pollinated. **LONGEVITY** Up to 80 years, but much more if coppiced.

 Hazelnuts are edible and gorgeous.

 Often coppiced for its pliable wood, used for hurdles and thatching.

 In central England, the tree now flowers a month earlier than 50 years ago.

TOP, LEFT TO RIGHT: *OFTEN MULTI-STEMMED; TYPICAL LEAF; NUT RIPENING.*

ABOVE: *PLUMP BUD*

BELOW LEFT: *FEMALE FLOWERS*

BELOW RIGHT: *MALE CATKINS*

JAN	FEB	MAR	APR	MAY	JUN	JUL	AUG	SEP	OCT	NOV	DEC

COMMON BEECH

Fagus sylvatica

Well-drained soils, especially on chalk. Widely planted. Native and common.

This is a big, bulky, bullying tree that often forms large stands of its own species. The broad, supremely elegant, curving and arching trunks and branches convey a very special, slightly surreal atmosphere to a beechwood, as if every tree was sculpted. The leaves form a dense canopy, leaving a summer beechwood dark and empty and without a herb layer on the ground. Young trees and those used for hedges are unusual for keeping their brown dead leaves on the twigs in winter. It is a large deciduous tree, usually to 30m tall.

One of the region's few trees that is easily identified by its bark. The leaves, fruits and buds are also distinctive, but the flowers are easy to miss completely. **BARK** Most unusually smooth and greyish, even in large, old trees. There may be some etchings and dots, usually arranged horizontally (letters and other markings are the work of vandals and lovers). **LEAVES** Oval, each with a pointed tip, and with obvious veins but no teeth. They have wavy margins

tall and broad

ABOVE & LEFT: *THE TREE IN WINTER AND SUMMER*

and young leaves have hairy tips. Leaves 4–9cm long. **FRUITS** Rough, with a woody cup covered with bristles, 12–18mm long. **BUDS** Long and pointed (torpedo-like) and, unusually, stick well out at an angle from the twig (twigs are often zigzagging). **FLOWERS** Easily missed. Male flowers grow in blobby, fluffy catkins that hang down. Females in pairs, erect, and looking like wigs.

ABOVE LEFT: *LEAF WITH WAVY MARGINS*

ABOVE CENTRE: *SMOOTH GREY BARK*

ABOVE RIGHT: *BEECH BUD*

BELOW: *MALE CATKINS*

 Male and female flowers are separate but on the same tree. **SEEDS** Triangular nuts within bristly fruits. Dispersed by birds and mammals. **FLOWERS** Wind pollinated. **LONGEVITY** Usually to 150–200 years, but sometimes more.

 The tree is fantastic for hedges.

 About 10 per cent of France's forests are of this tree.

 In late spring, the trees drop leaves that are too shaded to be of any use.

FACT FILE

FAMILY Fagaceae (Beeches & Oaks) HEIGHT Maximum 40m
SIMILAR SPECIES Hornbeam (p. 66).

| JAN | FEB | MAR | APR | MAY | JUN | JUL | AUG | SEP | OCT | NOV | DEC |

SWEET CHESTNUT

Castanea sativa

Woodland and parkland. Mainly planted. Native to southern Europe. Probably introduced to Britain in Roman times but only recently to the Netherlands.

BELOW LEFT: *TRUNK OFTEN TWISTED*

BELOW CENTRE: *LEAVES WITH 'CUTTING' EDGES*

BELOW RIGHT: *FULSOME YELLOWISH CATKINS*

Justifiably appreciated for its wonderful autumn chestnuts, this tree is a native of southern Europe, introduced to northern Europe. In summer its huge leaves provide welcome shade, and in autumn they are tinted a gorgeous golden-orange colour. Sweet Chestnuts have particularly broad limbs, and some can grow enormous girths, as wide as 2m, and form into weird, alien shapes. The wood is ideal for coppicing into poles.

The unusual leaves are unmistakable, while the fruits are proverbial. Check the flowers, bark and buds, too. **LEAVES** Huge (16–28cm long) and have ferocious-looking serrated edges, as if you could use them as saws. The spikes coincide with the ends of the veins. No other leaves look like them. **FRUITS** Nuts encased in a fiercely spiky casing, like a sea urchin; it really can hurt when you pick up a nut while foraging. The nuts look like conkers from a Horse Chestnut (p. 124) but are much smaller, just 5–7cm across. **FLOWERS** Long, frothy yellowish catkins that look like pipe cleaners. There are multiple spikes on each twig, each 12–20cm long, and they colour the whole tree. On

FACT FILE

FAMILY Fagaceae (Beeches & Oaks) HEIGHT Maximum 36m SIMILAR SPECIES Superficially similar to other large woodland trees.

often tall with bulky limbs

ABOVE & RIGHT: *THE TREE IN WINTER AND SUMMER*

spike, male flowers are at the tip, female ones below. **BARK** Very deeply vertically fissured. In older trees it can look spiralled or corkscrewed, as if a giant had tried to twist the tree. **BUDS** Appear to sit on their own 'shelf' or 'plinth'.

 Male and female flowers occur in different parts of the same catkin. **SEEDS** The chestnuts, 1–3 per fruit. **FLOWERS** Insect pollinated. **LONGEVITY** To 600 years.

BELOW: *FALLEN SEEDS IN CASING*

 These are the spiky-covered chestnuts you find on the woodland floor in autumn and are delicious roasted in the oven; cooked ones can sometimes be bought on street corners. Timber is excellent for furniture making.

 Flowers apparently smell of frying mushrooms.

 Spiky covering of fruits is made up from modified leaves.

| JAN | FEB | MAR | APR | MAY | JUN | JUL | AUG | SEP | OCT | NOV | DEC |

PEDUNCULATE OAK

Quercus robur

Mainly on deep, rich soils such as clay, avoiding upland areas. Often planted in hedges. May form its own woods. Native and abundant.

If there is one tree that everybody should learn to recognize it is surely this one – the mighty and most dominant tree in much of the lowlands of the region. It is a wonderful symbol of permanence, strength and small things (acorns) producing mighty results (massive trees). The landscape is littered with old trees (veteran oaks), many past their best, reassuringly still going and keeping untold secrets. There is nothing quite as enveloping as an oakwood in summer, the leaves and limbs bursting with life, the bird song soothing, the canopy a mystery. This oak is a large deciduous tree with a broad crown and many branches.

 When present, the famous leaves have the proverbial oak shape. Also take note of the fruits, bark, flowers and buds. **LEAVES** These are lobed. The lobes are uneven and deep. At the base, the stalk is clothed with two small lobes, leaving less than 1cm of stalk exposed. Leaves 10–12cm long, 7–8cm wide. **FRUITS** Acorns, the seed in a small cup (cupule). Groups of acorns are on a stalk, 2–9cm long (see Sessile Oak, p. 76). The long

massive trunk and branches

ABOVE & LEFT: *THE TREE IN WINTER AND SUMMER*

stalk is called a peduncle, hence the name of the tree. **BARK** Invariably very rugged and old looking, with vertical fissures and multiple knobs and burrs. **FLOWERS** Male flowers yellow-green catkins that hang down like net curtains in the canopy. Male catkins 2–4cm long. Female flowers minute, just 2mm long, brown, and at ends of shoots. **BUDS** Distinctively, very clustered at the tips of twigs. Reddish. Fewer than 20 scales per bud (more than 20 in the Sessile Oak).

Male and female parts occur on the same tree. **SEEDS** Acorns, set in a cupule. Acorns 1.5–4cm long, and dispersed by animals. **FLOWERS** Wind pollinated. **LONGEVITY** Maximum about 1,000 years.

The famously durable wood has been used for almost anything, from Viking longboats to fighting warships.

There is one good crop of acorns approximately every other year.

In Britain, the wood was once used exclusively in medieval timber-framed buildings and for shipbuilding.

ABOVE LEFT: RUGGED TRUNK

ABOVE CENTRE: UNSTALKED LEAF

ABOVE RIGHT: MALE FLOWERS

BELOW: ACORNS ON STALK

FACT FILE

FAMILY Fagaceae (Beeches & Oaks) **HEIGHT** Maximum 45m **SIMILAR SPECIES** Sessile Oak and many other planted oak species. Also known as the English Oak.

JAN	FEB	MAR	APR	MAY	JUN	JUL	AUG	SEP	OCT	NOV	DEC

SESSILE OAK

Quercus petraea

On poorer soils than Pedunculate Oak, and often at higher altitudes. Native and abundant.

Most people think there is only one majestic oak tree forming the landscape of Britain and northern Europe, but in fact there are two very similar species. This is the overlooked one, although in many places it is the dominant tree, forming large woodlands of its own, especially in poorer, more acidic soils and in upland areas with higher rainfall. The Sessile Oak presents a neat contrast to its cousin: Pedunculate Oaks have short leaf stalks and long acorn stalks, while Sessile Oaks have long leaf stalks and short acorn stalks. You just have to remember which way round it is. This is a large tree with a domed crown, to about 40m in height. It often has a straighter trunk than the Pedunculate Oak (p. 74).

BELOW: *BUDS BUNCHED AT END OF SHOOT*

 Best distinguished from the Pedunculate Oak by its leaves and fruits. Also check the buds, bark and flowers. **LEAVES** Typical oak-shape leaves; well lobed; 7–14cm long, 4–8cm wide. Stalks about 1.2–2cm long (compare with the Pedunculate Oak). They are also larger and glossier than those of the Pedunculate Oak. **FRUITS** Acorns not stalked (or have 1–2mm stalks). Each acorn 2–3cm long. **BARK** Brown and deeply fissured, like Pedunculate Oak's, but tree is often taller and less excessively branched. **FLOWERS** Drooping yellow-green

well-lobed leaves

acorns without stalks

FACT FILE

FAMILY Fagaceae (Beeches & Oaks) **HEIGHT** Maximum 42m **SIMILAR SPECIES** Pedunculate Oak and other planted oaks of many species. Also known as the Durmast Oak.

ABOVE & RIGHT: *THE TREE IN WINTER AND SUMMER*

male catkins 2–4cm long. Female flowers minute, just 2mm long, brown, and at ends of shoots. **BUDS** As on the Pedunculate Oak, bunched at the end of the twig. However, Sessile Oak buds have more than 20 scales.

 Male and female parts occur on the same tree. **SEEDS** Acorns, set in a cupule; dispersed by animals. **FLOWERS** Male catkins wind pollinated. **LONGEVITY** Maximum about 1,200 years (older when pollarded).

 The wood is used for a great deal of construction, including fences.

 In Britain, about 400 species of animal are dependent on oaks.

BELOW LEFT: *DARK BROWN, DEEPLY FISSURED BARK*

BELOW RIGHT: *DEVELOPING ACORNS*

| JAN | FEB | MAR | APR | MAY | JUN | JUL | AUG | SEP | OCT | NOV | DEC |

EVERGREEN OAK

Quercus ilex

The idea of an oak tree that does not drop its leaves in autumn feels odd, somehow. But the Evergreen Oak, a tree from the Mediterranean region, shows that curious combination of acorns and almost Holly-like dark green leaves that persist throughout the winter and add some much-needed green to the landscape. It is planted for shelter, especially near the sea, but it also spreads by itself, especially in warmer places. It is a large, dense tree that generally grows to 25m.

Planted in many areas, but does best in warmer parts.

BELOW: *DARK, HOLLY-LIKE LEAVES*

The leaves are most obvious; also check the fruits, flowers and bark. **LEAVES** Glossy dark green with crinkled edges that can, at times, be spiny like the leaves of a Holly (p. 128), especially on young trees, and fairly hard to the touch They are hairy beneath, and 4–8cm long. **FRUITS** Acorns in a cupule. Unlike in 'normal' oaks, they are deeper seated in the cup, less than halfway out. They are also smaller (1–2cm long), with a pointed tip. **FLOWERS** Greenish-yellow catkins that dominate the canopy in June, as the previous year's leaves start to fall. Male catkins 2–4cm long. Female flowers minute and catkin-like; much shorter than male catkins. **BARK** Dark grey and scaly. **TWIGS** Hairy. **BUDS** very small, clustered and hairy.

large spreading tree

 Male and female parts occur on the same tree. **SEEDS** Acorns, set in a cupule; dispersed by animals. **FLOWERS** Wind pollinated. **LONGEVITY** About 400 years.

FACT FILE

FAMILY Fagaceae (Beeches & Oaks) **HEIGHT** Maximum 28m **SIMILAR SPECIES** Vaguely similar to the Holly, and eucalyptuses (p. 90). Also known as the Holm Oak (Holm=Holly).

JAN	FEB	MAR	APR	MAY	JUN	JUL	AUG	SEP	OCT	NOV	DEC

TURKEY OAK

Quercus cerris

broad crown

This oak from southern Europe has found the region to its liking and, in Britain at least, since being introduced in the eighteenth century it has become more and more common, taking over in some places, especially on sandy soils. Unfortunately, it has brought an unwelcome passenger, the Knopper Gall Wasp, which lays its eggs in Pedunculate Oak (p. 74) acorns as well as its own, adversely affecting the native species. The Turkey Oak is a large deciduous tree with a broad crown, usually to 30m tall.

Introduced from southern Europe, planted widely and, in Britain at least, thoroughly naturalized. Thrives on sandy and acid soils.

ABOVE: *ACORNS FIT INTO 'MOSSY' CUP*

BELOW: *SHINY LEAVES WITH SQUARE-CUT LOBES*

 Easily distinguished from other oaks by its fruits and, to some extent, its leaves. **FRUITS** Acorns are large (2.5–4cm long) and each fits into a 'mossy' cupule. **LEAVES** Like a cross between Holly (p. 128) and oak leaves, with more square-cut lobes, but very variable, with lots of lobes. They are fairly shiny and rough, but are deciduous, turning yellow; 7–14cm long, 3–5cm wide. **FLOWERS** Male catkins 2–4cm long. Female flowers minute, catkin-like and much shorter. **BUDS** Have remarkable curling strands, like string on top. **BARK** Dark and closely fissured, with some cracks almost orange.

 Male and female parts occur on the same tree. **SEEDS** Acorns set in a cupule; dispersed by animals. **FLOWERS** Wind pollinated. **LONGEVITY** About 800 years.

 Looks pretty, but the timber is dreadful.

FACT FILE

FAMILY Fagaceae (Beeches & Oaks) HEIGHT Maximum 40m SIMILAR SPECIES Other oaks.

JAN	FEB	MAR	APR	MAY	JUN	JUL	AUG	SEP	OCT	NOV	DEC

WYCH ELM

Ulmus glabra

Woods and hedgerows. Prefers moist soils, but also limestone. Native. Most common in the north and mountains.

Sadly, this tree is a case of the mighty falling. Found over much of Europe, growing tall and especially thriving beside rivers and in mountains, the population of this beautiful tree has been severely ravaged by the latest outbreaks of Dutch Elm Disease since the 1970s. The tree is very susceptible as soon as its trunk and branches grow broad enough to be of interest to Elm Bark Beetles, which spread the lethal fungus. In contrast to other elms, the Wych Elm only spreads by seed, not producing root suckers. The Wych Elm is a large, spreading deciduous tree with a round outline, usually growing to 35m in height.

 Most easily identified in season by the leaves, but the fruits and flowers are also unusual. **LEAVES** Elm leaves are unusual for being non-symmetrical, with one side arising from the stalk before the other at the base, which makes the central vein look offset. The leaves are oval, alternate on the stem and 7–16cm long. They also taper steeply to a sharp point. They are sharply toothed and have very obvious veins (12–18 pairs), and are roughly hairy on both sides. **FRUITS** Each flattened into a round samara, a papery disc 1.5cm across, the

BELOW LEFT: *PAPERY FRUITS PACKED TOGETHER*

BELOW RIGHT: *TYPICAL, NON-SYMMETRICAL LEAF*

FACT FILE

FAMILY Ulmaceae (Elms) HEIGHT Maximum 40m SIMILAR SPECIES Other elm species, Hornbeam and Common Beech (pp. 66 and 70).

ABOVE: *FLOWERS*

BELOW & RIGHT:
*THE TREE IN
WINTER AND
SUMMER*

*feathery
foliage*

aerodynamic wing surrounding the centrally placed seed like the white of a fried egg surrounding the yolk (see Field Elm, p. 82). The samaras are packed together like a bunch of prawn crackers. Shed June onwards. **FLOWERS** Somewhat pitiful (2cm wide), petal-less tufts of reddish stamens, produced before the leaves. **TRUNK** Often broad and short below the lowest branches. **BARK** Very rugged, with lots of vertical ridges and cracks. **BUDS** Small, blackish and hairy.

ABOVE: *SMALL BUDS*

Flowers are hermaphrodite, with male and female parts. **SEEDS** Contained within the samara. **FRUITS** Winged samaras wind dispersed, shed from June onwards. **FLOWERS** Wind pollinated. **LONGEVITY** Potentially 400 years, but see above.

Elm wood was often used for coffins and other furniture, such as stools. Elm limbs had a reputation for breaking off suddenly, potentially providing use for the former.

When the Wych Elm first recolonized Britain after the last ice age, beginning about 9,500 years ago, it progressed at a rate of 500m per year.

JAN	FEB	MAR	APR	MAY	JUN	JUL	AUG	SEP	OCT	NOV	DEC

Found in hedgerows and woodland edges. Native and fairly common.

FIELD ELM

Ulmus minor

Field Elms are the smaller elms of the region, these days often appearing only as suckers before they are killed by Dutch Elm Disease. It is a sad fate for a tree that was, in Britain, more common than any other tree in the landscape. Field Elm is a blanket term referring to a number of subspecies, hybrids and clones that have the botanists drooling, but their obscure differences are a nightmare for the rest of us. The Field Elm is a medium-sized tree with a domed shape, to about 30m tall. It often suckers.

BELOW & RIGHT: *THE TREE IN WINTER AND SUMMER*

 Best distinguished from the Wych Elm (p. 80) by its leaves and fruits. **LEAVES** Characteristic elm shape, not symmetrical, but with one side of the leaf 'ahead' of the other connecting to the central stem. Smaller and rounder than Wych Elm leaves (3–7cm long, not 7–16cm). Also have fewer veins (7–12, not 12–18), and are much less hairy, if hairy at all. In some forms the leaves are almost circular. May have a longer stalk. **FRUITS** Paper-thin aerodynamic wings. Seeds pink and, in this species, set close to the end of the samara, near the notch (not in the middle). **FLOWERS** Small cups of reddish anthers, looking like a trifle ice-cream. Despite their small size (2mm wide), they colour the tree pink in late winter. **TWIGS** Always hairy (in the Wych Elm only when young). **BARK** Greyish and very roughly wrinkled and notched. **BUDS** Hairless, in contrast to those of the Wych Elm.

ABOVE LEFT: *SMALL, HAIRLESS BUDS*

ABOVE CENTRE: *NON-SYMMETRICAL LEAF, ROUNDER THAN WYCH ELM*

ABOVE RIGHT: *REDDISH FLOWERS*

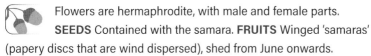 Flowers are hermaphrodite, with male and female parts. **SEEDS** Contained with the samara. **FRUITS** Winged 'samaras' (papery discs that are wind dispersed), shed from June onwards. **FLOWERS** Wind pollinated. **LONGEVITY** At least 400 years.

 The wood is often used in boat building.

 124 species of insect and mite have been recorded feeding on elms, making them a rich habitat.

FACT FILE

FAMILY Ulmaceae (Elms) HEIGHT Maximum 33m SIMILAR SPECIES Wych Elm and Common Hazel (p. 68). The European White Elm *U. laevis* is common on the Continent. It is mainly a waterside species and has particularly asymmetrical leaves.

JAN	FEB	MAR	APR	MAY	JUN	JUL	AUG	SEP	OCT	NOV	DEC

BLACK MULBERRY

Morus nigra

Planted in gardens and parks, and often naturalized on waste ground and in other places. Introduced.

Mulberries have been cultivated for so long that nobody knows quite where they came from originally, although south-west Asia is the most probable source. They are now found worldwide in warmer regions, although they do quite well in our region, especially in sunny corners of cottage gardens and in parks. Mulberries are also associated with silk moths, but their main food plant is actually a relative, the White Mulberry *M. alba*. This is a small deciduous tree, often as broad as it is tall, growing to about 12m.

BELOW: *BERRIES*

 Readily identified by its famous fruits, as well as its trunk, bark and leaves. **FRUITS** Look like raspberries, albeit more elongated, and grow right on the stem. They start green, go red and finally turn purple, usually not until August. Technically a mass of drupes; 1.5cm long. **FLOWERS** In small catkins with downy stalks, yellowish-green, male 2.5cm; female like small tentacles from central green 'body', 1cm long. **TRUNK** and **BARK** Always look old and gnarled and knotted, even when young, with a distinct reddish-brown hue. **LEAVES** Truly fulsome, large and heart shaped; definitely tropical looking. They have teeth. Hairy, especially below. Each 6–20cm long. **BUDS** Purple, short and sharp.

 Male and female flowers borne on same plant. **SEEDS** Very small, each inside a single drupe, dispersed by animals. **LONGEVITY** 500–1,000 years.

 The edible berries are gorgeous.

branches have a mazy complexity

FACT FILE

FAMILY Moraceae (Mulberries) HEIGHT Maximum 14m SIMILAR SPECIES None.

JAN	FEB	MAR	APR	MAY	JUN	JUL	AUG	SEP	OCT	NOV	DEC

MAGNOLIA

Magnolia spp.

Magnolias are such an important part of the late-winter garden and neighbourhood scene in most towns and villages in the region that it is perhaps surprising that they are not native. The nearest they occur naturally is in the Americas, but who could envisage the cold months of late winter without their beautiful flowers? They are thought to be primitive plants, around since the time of the dinosaurs, about 95 million years ago. The petals and sepals look the same so are indistinguishable. Magnolias are trees or large shrubs, usually to 20m tall; some are evergreen.

These are garden plants, planted in parks and amenity areas. Introduced from south-east Asia or the Americas.

ABOVE: *LARGE LEAVES FOR SIZE OF TREE*

BELOW: *THE TULIP-LIKE BLOOMS*

Most easily identified by the flowers. Also check the buds, leaves and bark. **FLOWERS** Large, cup-like blooms. They are usually creamy-white, purple or mauve, and stand upright on the stems. They are arranged in whorls and can be 10–30cm broad. **BUDS** Huge and look like exotic-coloured light bulbs. Early on, they look as though they are covered in cobwebs. **LEAVES** Large (up to 30cm long), and simple, without teeth. **BARK** Grey and smooth on younger plants. **FRUITS** Cone-like stalks, with scales, from which the seeds drop.

Male and female parts occur on each flower. **SEEDS** Dispersed from fruits in situ. **FLOWERS** Pollinated by insects. **LONGEVITY** 80–120 years.

FACT FILE

FAMILY Magnoliaceae (Magnolias) HEIGHT Maximum 30m SIMILAR SPECIES Emerging buds of the Common Whitebeam (p.104) similar to those of magnolias.

JAN	FEB	MAR	APR	MAY	JUN	JUL	AUG	SEP	OCT	NOV	DEC

TULIP TREE

Liriodendron tulipifera

Mainly planted in parks and other open spaces. Native to North America.

Introduced from North America, it is a magnificent, towering, extraordinary species, with unique flowers and leaves. It is a relic of times past, from a group best represented in the Cretaceous period some 100 million years ago. It is the tallest tree in eastern North America and grows up to 36m in Europe.

ABOVE: *THE LEAVES RESEMBLE BUTTERFLY WINGS*

BELOW: *CUP-SHAPED FLOWER*

The leaves are unique among all trees, while the flowers do indeed look like tulips, although they are closer in form to those of magnolias (p. 85). **LEAVES** On long stalks, oddly square and symmetrical; 12–15cm across. **FLOWERS** Delicate pale green and orange. Cup-shaped with six petals about 5cm across. **BARK** Pale grey and neatly furrowed. Ridges criss-cross like strands of string. **FRUITS** Dark brown cones, like closed cups of spent tulips, 3–5cm tall; not easy to see. Made from narrow scales, like onion peel.

Flowers are both male and female. **SEEDS** Attached to wings within fruit 'cone', dispersed by the wind. **LONGEVITY** Up to 500 years.

Native Americans have long used the wood for dugout canoes.

FACT FILE

FAMILY Magnoliaceae (Magnolias) HEIGHT Maximum 58m SIMILAR SPECIES Superficially like a poplar (pp. 46–53).

JAN	FEB	MAR	APR	MAY	JUN	JUL	AUG	SEP	OCT	NOV	DEC

BAY

Laurus nobilis

The Bay Tree is a dense evergreen tree or shrub, to about 18m tall. It is one of those plants that keeps on giving, principally due to the aromatic nature of its leaves, which are used as herbs in cookery. Its foliage is also superb for clipping and creating topiary. The Romans used bay leaves to make garlands for notable people.

Planted widely in gardens and parks, mainly in warmer areas. Introduced from the Mediterranean.

 Easily identified by its leaves, unusual flowers, berries and bark. **LEAVES** Evergreen, leathery and heavily fruity scented. They are 5–12cm long, each one fairly narrow with a long point, and crinkled edges. **FLOWERS** Only 1cm across, and densely clustered near the stem. They are cream coloured with four petals. **FRUITS** Round, black berries (technically drupes), 1.2cm across, becoming glossy. **BARK** Unusually smooth and grey.

dense evergreen

 Male and female parts grow on different plants. **SEEDS** Single within each fruit. **LONGEVITY** 50–150 years.

 Ground Bay leaves are often put into the cocktail Bloody Mary.

 Once a key component of the laurel forests that covered much of the Mediterranean, 50 million years ago.

ABOVE: *SMOOTH, GREY BARK*

BELOW: *SMALL, CREAMY FLOWERS*

FACT FILE

FAMILY Lauraceae (Laurels) HEIGHT Maximum 20m SIMILAR SPECIES Other evergreen shrubs such as the Cherry Laurel (p. 117), Rhododendron (p. 127) and even Holly (p. 128).

JAN	FEB	MAR	APR	MAY	JUN	JUL	AUG	SEP	OCT	NOV	DEC

LONDON PLANE

Platanus x acerifolia

Planted widely, especially in parks and streets. Introduced and common.

The London Plane, a large, broad-crowned tree 30m or more in height, is a hybrid between the Oriental Plane *P. orientalis* and the American Buttonwood *P. occidentalis*, but no one is exactly sure where it first emerged. From its inauspicious beginning, this striking, tall, flaking barked tree has found its way around the world, particularly to cities, where it is highly resistant to air pollution and the cramped space for its roots. It is abundant in the centre of London, as well as New York, Johannesburg, Buenos Aires and Sydney.

ABOVE: *DISTINCTIVE FLAKING BARK*

Unusually, this tree is best identified by its bark, although the fruits are very distinctive, and the leaves are large. **BARK** An amazing smooth cream and grey, with very obvious peeling plates. It is unlike that of any other tree. **FRUITS** Like pompoms on strings, or meat balls when they go brown. There are 2–6, or sometimes more, per string. Close up, they can be seen to be made up from hundreds of compartments with hooks on the outside. They are about 3cm across. **LEAVES** Large, each with five lobes, similar to those of a maple or Sycamore (p. 122); however, they are alternate along the stem, not opposite. Each lobe has sharp teeth. Leaves 10–20cm long and 12–25cm

maple-like leaves

fruits like pom-poms

FACT FILE

FAMILY Platanaceae (Planes) HEIGHT Maximum 44m SIMILAR SPECIES Leaves vaguely Sycamore-like.

broad, with stalk up to 10cm long. **FLOWERS** Barely visible round heads at ends of stems.

 Male and female flowers are on the same tree but on different stems. **SEEDS** Within the hanging fruits, which break up for the wind to disperse the seeds, carried by the hairs. **FRUITS** Break up in spring. **LONGEVITY** At least 320 years.

 Mainly an ornamental.

 The breaking up of the seed balls in spring can trigger asthma attacks in some people.

JAN	FEB	MAR	APR	MAY	JUN	JUL	AUG	SEP	OCT	NOV	DEC

EUCALYPTUS

Eucalyptus spp.

Planted everywhere, in parks, gardens and plantations. Introduced from Australia.

The eucalypts, or gum trees, are a large group of evergreen trees and shrubs that make up a major part of the Australian tree flora – there are more *Eucalyptus* species around Sydney than all of Britain's native trees put together. They are trees or shrubs of varying height and habit, growing to 30m plus. Fast-growing and aromatic, with attractive foliage and flowers, they are enormously popular – and also easy to recognize.

Easily identified by the leaves and bark. The flowers vary.
LEAVES Variable. Evergreen but look like those of deciduous trees, not conifers. They are also much paler, often bluey-green. Notice how they hang directly down (to avoid the glare of the Australian sun). They are also non-symmetrical, bending one way,

BELOW: *BUDS ARE LIKE CAPSULES*

grey-green foliage

like bananas. Many are fairly narrow. **BARK** Variable, but there are always bits stripping away, often showing light brown beneath. **BUDS** Extraordinary, looking like sealed cups. They split open to reveal a mass of stamens, of various colours according to the species, and like the tentacles of a sea anemone, or even the bristles of a brush.

 Male and female parts occur in the same flower. **SEEDS** Disperse by dropping from the fruits on the tree. **FRUITS** Hard woody pods. **LONGEVITY** More than 200 years.

 Eucalypts release an oil that is a powerful disinfectant.

⭐ Eucalypt flowers are rich in nectar, so are a powerful attractant to insects.

ABOVE LEFT: *STAMENS DEVELOPED FROM BUDS*

ABOVE RIGHT: *TRUNK PEELS, LEAVING BROWN SECTIONS*

BELOW: *LEAVES OFTEN BEND ONE WAY*

FACT FILE

FAMILY Myrtaceae (Myrtles) HEIGHT Maximum in Australia to 100m. SIMILAR SPECIES Possibly the Common Ash (p. 146).

JAN	FEB	MAR	APR	MAY	JUN	JUL	AUG	SEP	OCT	NOV	DEC

COMMON HAWTHORN

Crataegus monogyna

Woodland, scrub, bare ground and hedges. Native and abundant.

This deciduous shrub, 2–15m tall, varies enormously, and is sometimes multi-stemmed. In much of the region this is the most common hedgerow shrub. It thrives almost anywhere in the open but tends to be replaced in shade and woodland by the Midland Hawthorn (p. 94). An extraordinarily dense bush, it is perfect for nesting birds as well as for defining boundaries. The brilliant white blossom (the pink cultivars are usually those of the Midland Hawthorn) is at its best in May – in Britain, the plant itself is often simply called the May. In autumn the crop of 'haws' is essential for migrant birds.

BELOW: *THE TREE IN WINTER AND SUMMER*

Densely branched tree with distinctive leaves, flowers and fruits. Also look at the bark, twigs and buds. **LEAVES** Rather rough and unique: small but deeply lobed. They usually look as though they have been cut halfway to the centre of the leaf, but sometimes the 'tear' reaches the midrib. There are 3–5 (–7) lobes, and all are toothed at the tip. Leaves 15–50mm long.

FLOWERS Grow in flat-topped clusters, which can absolutely dominate a bush. They are fragrant and attract many insects. Each flower is five petalled, 4–6mm in diameter, gleaming white and dotted with the male anthers. Single style in the middle distinguishes it from a Midland Hawthorn. **FRUITS** Known as 'haws', and are fleshy crimson cups 8–10mm in diameter. They are similar to rose hips but rounder. **BARK** Grey-brown and flaky, often with rectangular shapes. **TWIGS** Contain thorns and are red-brown (green at first). Spines emerge from the same point as the buds. Twigs often zigzag. **BUDS** Small and oval.

ABOVE LEFT: *GREY-BROWN, FLAKY BARK*

ABOVE CENTRE: *UNUSUAL LEAF, DEEPLY CUT*

ABOVE RIGHT: *THE CRIMSON HAWS*

Male and female parts are on the same flower. They need to be pollinated by another plant. **SEEDS** Single seed in each fruit (occasionally two). **FRUITS** In moderate-sized clusters; dispersed by birds and other animals. **FLOWERS** Pollinated by flies and other insects. **LONGEVITY** Up to 400 years.

BELOW LEFT: *THE FIVE-PETALLED FLOWERS*

BELOW: *SMALL, OVAL BUDS*

The fresh leaves, flowers and haws are all edible.

The Hethel Old Thorn 'nature reserve' in Norfolk, Britain, consists of just one Common Hawthorn tree.

FACT FILE

FAMILY Rosaceae (Roses) HEIGHT Maximum 15m SIMILAR SPECIES Midland Hawthorn (hybrids are frequent). Other shrubs with white blossom such as the Blackthorn (p. 112).

JAN	FEB	MAR	APR	MAY	JUN	JUL	AUG	SEP	OCT	NOV	DEC

MIDLAND HAWTHORN

Crataegus laevigata

The Midland Hawthorn is a shrub or small tree to 10m tall, which suffers from being compared to a more famous relative, in this case the Common Hawthorn (p. 92). It is, however, very much its own tree, unless it hybridizes with the Common Hawthorn and produces plants with intermediate properties, a fact of life to trouble tree identifiers. It is much more of a woodland plant than its light-loving relative, tolerating shade and often occurring in very old stands. It produces blossom and berries very similar to those of the Common Hawthorn.

Woodland and hedges. Often found in older hedgerows and ancient woods in Britain. Native and fairly common.

 Most easily identified by its leaves and flowers. **LEAVES** Small (2–6cm long) and lobed in characteristic hawthorn fashion, but they only have three rather shallow lobes, and these are not cut very deep, and certainly never to the midrib, but they are toothed. They

BELOW: *BROAD FLOWERS*

FACT FILE

FAMILY Rosaceae (Roses) HEIGHT Maximum 10m SIMILAR SPECIES Common Hawthorn. Other blossom trees with flat-topped sets of blooms, such as the Elder (p. 152).

a tree of the woodland community

have the shape of a three-toed animal footprint. **FLOWERS** Similar to flowers of the Common Hawthorn but have two to three styles (see detail in photograph), not one; 5–8mm long. They are slightly broader (petals 5–8mm rather than 4–6mm). Pink-flowered hawthorn cultivars are usually this species, not the Common Hawthorn. **FRUITS** Familiar shiny red haws, 8–10mm in length. **TWIGS** Less stiff and spiny than the Common Hawthorn's.

BELOW: *NOTE THE 2-3 GREEN STYLES*

 Male and female occur on the same flowers. **SEEDS** Two (sometimes three) in each fruit. **FRUITS** Eaten by birds and mammals and dispersed by them. **FLOWERS** Pollinated by insects, especially flies. **LONGEVITY** About 400 years.

 The stems are sometimes carved into walking sticks.

 The flowerheads are dense and flat so that insect pollinators can simply walk from one head to the next.

JAN	FEB	MAR	APR	MAY	JUN	JUL	AUG	SEP	OCT	NOV	DEC

WILD PEAR

Pyrus communis

Hedges, parks, gardens, waste ground and woodland edges. Origin unknown.

The Wild Pear is a medium-sized deciduous tree that is to 20m tall. It is not unusual to find it in the countryside, but delve into the origins of the species and the picture soon gets murky. It turns out that just about every plant that can be found has grown from discarded pear seeds or was planted as part of an orchard. Nobody seems entirely sure whether Wild Pears and cultivated pears are any different from each other. Still, who really cares when the fruits taste as good as they do?

 Not surprisingly, the fruits are the obvious giveaway. Also check the flowers, leaves and bark. **FRUITS** Pear shaped. Those of the 'wilder' forms may be only up to 4cm long and surprisingly round (cultivated form up to 12cm); they are also quite hard and not very sweet. Others look just like normal pears. They ripen to a golden-yellow. **FLOWERS** Stunningly pure white and can produce some of the finest blossom anywhere. They grow in clusters (corymbs), each 2–3cm across, with five petals. Anthers are purple and add speckles to the white. **LEAVES** Plush and rounded, and glossier than Apple leaves (p. 100). Base can be expanded into a heart shape, but it varies. Leaves 3–8cm long. **TWIGS** Usually not spiny. **BARK** Brown and has the

BELOW LEFT: *BARK WITH CLOSE FISSURES*

BELOW CENTRE: *LEAF TYPICALLY GLOSSY*

BELOW RIGHT: *THE WILD PEAR FRUIT IS SLIGHTLY SMALLER THAN THE CULTIVATED*

FACT FILE

FAMILY Rosaceae (Roses) HEIGHT Maximum 20m SIMILAR SPECIES Apples and other blossom trees.

medium-sized tree

ABOVE: *THE BUDS*

appearance of shattered shards of wood. **BUDS** Dark brown and pointed like a blunt pencil.

 Male and female are within same flower. **SEEDS** Within fleshy fruits, eaten and dispersed by animals. **LONGEVITY** About 250 years.

The wood is used for woodwind instruments and kitchen utensils.

★ Archaeological evidence suggests that Europeans have been consuming pears since the Neolithic period (up to 10,000 years ago).

TRUE WILD PEAR
Pyrus pyraster
In theory, 'true' Wild Pears differ from cultivated pears by having spines, smaller and less fleshy fruits, which are often simply globular, smaller leaves (4cm) and greyish twigs.

JAN	FEB	MAR	APR	MAY	JUN	JUL	AUG	SEP	OCT	NOV	DEC

CRAB APPLE

Malus sylvestris

Usually on woodland edges or in hedges. Native. Generally not very common.

The sight of the yellow fruits carpeting the ground beneath this tree is a sure sign that it is the relatively unloved Crab Apple, not the juicy cultivated Apple (p. 100). The fruits are truly bitter and are usually used for making a jelly, often regarded as the best of its kind. Although native, this is not a common species and it is quite fussy, needing a lot of light and minimal competition. You tend to encounter it singly, or a few trees together. The Crab Apple is a small, spiny, deciduous tree, usually to 10m in height.

 Has easily recognized fruits and staggering flowers. Note also the leaves, bark and buds. **FRUITS** Like very small apples, globular and just 2–3cm in diameter, but usually yellow or yellow-green. They are hard to bite into and have a very sharp taste, so are almost inedible, completely lacking the gentle sweetness of cultivated apples. **FLOWERS** Blossom glorious in spring, a riot of white flowers tinged with an intoxicating deep

spiny tree with a 'messy' look

ABOVE & LEFT: *THE TREE IN WINTER AND SUMMER*

ABOVE: *OVAL LEAVES OFTEN LOOK 'TIRED'*

ABOVE RIGHT & RIGHT: *FRUITS USUALLY GREEN BUT CAN BE PURPLE*

pink, the colour of the flower buds. The flowers are in small clusters (cymes) of 4–6, with each flower 3–4cm across. **LEAVES** Distinctly oval, toothed and only 3–5cm long. Although glossy, they can soon look 'tired'. In contrast to those of a cultivated Apple, they are hairless (except when very young). **BARK** Deep purplish-brown with neat but irregular flecks. **TWIGS** Greyish and bear many short side shoots that give an untidy look. **BUDS** Reddish-brown and clustered.

BELOW: *BARK PALE PURPLISH-BROWN*

 Male and female are within the same flower. **SEEDS** Within the eaten fruits, dispersed by animals. **FLOWERS** Insect pollinated. **LONGEVITY** About 100 years.

 Often planted in orchards to keep the pollinators happy.

 Crab Apples often grow far apart, so that insect pollination is the only viable option for them.

FACT FILE

FAMILY Rosaceae (Roses) HEIGHT Maximum 17m SIMILAR SPECIES Cultivated Apple (p. 100) and other blossom trees.

JAN	FEB	MAR	APR	MAY	JUN	JUL	AUG	SEP	OCT	NOV	DEC

APPLE

Malus pumila

Hedges, scrub and waste places. Introduced long ago, and often naturalized.

If Apples had personalities, they would be people pleasers. How else can you explain the glorious fruits, produced in such prodigious quantities and in such perfect packages, as well as the wondrous display of early spring blossom and the general vigour? No wonder the Apple has been celebrated in many different cultures for thousands of years. The familiar Apple originates from Kazakhstan in Central Asia. Any Apple tree that you might see in a wild situation could arise from a vast range of crossbreeds and cultivars, of which there are thousands. This is a small deciduous tree without spines and with tangled branches, growing to 10m tall.

The fruits are the most familiar feature, but the flowers and leaves pay examination. **FRUITS** Everyone knows apples. The fruits are at least 4cm in diameter and often much larger (up to 12cm). **FLOWERS** Reach a height in May, covering the trees with abundant blossom. The flower buds are an intense pink at first. They are then white, retaining some pink, especially on the backs; 3–4cm across, in small clusters (cymes) of 4–6. **LEAVES** Quite large (up to 15cm long) and oval, with small but obvious teeth. They are downy underneath and

BELOW LEFT: *BARK GREY WITH CLOSE-SET SCALES*

BELOW CENTRE: *OVAL LEAVES*

BELOW RIGHT: *BLOSSOM SHOWING PINK FLOWER BUDS*

FACT FILE

FAMILY Rosaceae (Roses) HEIGHT Maximum 20m SIMILAR SPECIES Crab Apple and Wild Pear (p. 96).

small tree with glorious
spring blossom

on the stalk. **TWIGS** Not spiny (see Crab Apple,
p. 98). **BARK** Greyish, with a close-set scaly
pattern.

 Male and female are within the same
flower. **SEEDS** Dispersed by animals.
FLOWERS Insect pollinated. **LONGEVITY** About
20–25 years.

 As if we did not already love apples
enough, they are the ingredient used
for cider.

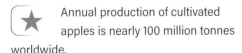 Annual production of cultivated
apples is nearly 100 million tonnes
worldwide.

ABOVE: *CLUSTERS OF
FRUIT*

JAN	FEB	MAR	APR	MAY	JUN	JUL	AUG	SEP	OCT	NOV	DEC

ROWAN

Sorbus aucuparia

Common and widespread on sandy or loamy soils, but also grown widely for ornament.

The Rowan, or Mountain Ash, is a small deciduous tree, compact dome shaped and 5–15m tall. It is a pioneer species that easily colonizes open and recently grazed uplands. Native to the Palearctic, from the UK to China, it is an exceptionally pretty tree, particularly in late summer when it becomes emblazoned with orange-red berries. The Rowan prefers the cooler regions of the northern hemisphere. It is most common in the north and west of the region and can be found at high altitudes. Nevertheless, it is highly adaptable, which has made it a popular species for planting in urban streets and parks.

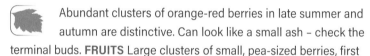 Abundant clusters of orange-red berries in late summer and autumn are distinctive. Can look like a small ash – check the terminal buds. **FRUITS** Large clusters of small, pea-sized berries, first

orange-red berries in autumn

green, turning orange, then ripening to bright scarlet. Loved by birds, including thrushes, waxwings and blackbirds. Edible to humans when cooked. Endure over winter. **LEAVES** Arranged in opposite pairs of up to 20cm long, comprising 4–8 pairs with a single terminal leaflet. Each leaflet elliptic with a toothed margin, and bright green in colour. Each leaf 7–16cm long. **FLOWERS** Dense, billowy clusters of small white flowers, each with five petals and long anthers. **BARK** Smooth and reddish-grey, with irregular, dark lenticels and light grey patches. **BUDS** Ovate, purple-brown and hairy.

ABOVE LEFT: HAIRY BUD

ABOVE RIGHT: FLOWER CLUSTER

BELOW: BERRY CLUSTER

Flowers contain both male and female reproductive parts and are pollinated by insects (the flowers are hermaphroditic). **SEEDS** Dispersed by animals – usually birds. **LONGEVITY** To about 200 years.

In medieval times the wood was used to make bows. When cooked, the tart berries make an excellent jelly and are rich in vitamin C.

According to legend, the Norse god Thor grabbed on to a Rowan tree when being swept down a river, thus saving him from being carried into the Underworld.

FACT FILE

FAMILY Rosaceae (Roses) HEIGHT Maximum 15m SIMILAR SPECIES Common Ash and Elder (pp. 146 and 152). Also known as the Mountain Ash.

JAN	FEB	MAR	APR	MAY	JUN	JUL	AUG	SEP	OCT	NOV	DEC

As a wild plant, mainly on chalk and limestone, in woods and scrub. Also abundantly planted on roadsides, in gardens and in amenity sites. Native.

COMMON WHITEBEAM

Sorbus aria

The name Whitebeam simply means 'White Tree', which is hardly imaginative, but at least sums up this luminous shrub of woodland edges and scrub. In spring, the whitish leaves look like magnolia flowers at first, then fold out to reveal their felty undersides, which make the tree glimmer in any breeze. This is a southern species, mainly found in chalk country. Not only is the foliage attractive, but the berries are a great favourite of birds in mid-autumn. This is a variable, medium-sized deciduous tree or shrub, usually to 15m in height. It is often multi-stemmed in the wild.

 The most obvious feature is the leaves, but also take note of the bark, flowers, berries and buds. **LEAVES** Frosty-white underneath in contrast to plain green above. In sunlight they look brilliant white due to the short hairs. Leaves oval and blunt, with irregular teeth, and heavily veined, 6–12cm in diameter. They turn orange in autumn. **BARK** Noticeably grey and relatively smooth. **FLOWERS** Sumptuous, wedding-dress white, in flat-topped clusters, each flower with five petals, 10–15mm across. **FRUITS** Scarlet berries in clusters with woody stalks. Relatively large, 11mm across. **BUDS** Oval with sharp tips, and green and brown.

BELOW LEFT: *GREY, SMOOTH BARK*

BELOW CENTRE: *HEAVILY VEINED LEAVES*

BELOW RIGHT: *LEAVES FROSTY-WHITE UNDERNEATH*

FACT FILE

FAMILY Rosaceae (Roses) HEIGHT Maximum 25m SIMILAR SPECIES Many other closely related whitebeam species; Swedish Whitebeam (p. 108).

ABOVE & RIGHT: *THE TREE IN WINTER AND SUMMER*

 Hermaphrodite, with male and female parts to each flower. **SEEDS** Two within each fruit, dispersed by birds. **FLOWERS** Pollinated by insects. **LONGEVITY** 70–100 years.

The wood was often used to make chairs and other furniture.

There are numerous related species of whitebeam, including many with extraordinarily small world ranges, sometimes just a few bushes hidden away on a single cliff-side in an obscure backwater.

BELOW LEFT: *LACY-WHITE FLOWERS*

BELOW RIGHT: *DEVELOPING FRUITS*

| JAN | FEB | MAR | APR | MAY | JUN | JUL | AUG | SEP | OCT | NOV | DEC |

Mainly found in clay and other basic soils, a component of woodlands. Localized. Native.

WILD SERVICE TREE

Sorbus torminalis

If ever a plant needed to hire a PR company, it would have to be the Wild Service Tree. It produces attractive flowers and very decent edible fruits and is quite easy to identify – yet these days hardly anyone knows about it. Only a few decades ago the fruit was sold in markets and, in Britain, pubs were named after it – the clue is the word 'chequers', an obsolete name for the tree. It is due a rebrand. Ecologists will tell you that it is an indicator of ancient woodland (woods that have been present as such for at least 400 years). This is a medium-sized, suckering deciduous tree, usually to 20m tall.

 Instantly recognizable fruits and easily identified leaves. Also note the flowers and buds. **FRUITS** Technically pomes, these look like spent rose-hips, with an unattractive brown colour. They are small (12–16mm across) and grow in clusters. Their surface is peppered with white spots. **LEAVES** Maple-like

ABOVE & LEFT: *THE TREE IN WINTER AND SUMMER*

(but alternate on the twig, whereas those of maples are in opposite pairs), with 3–5 pairs of lobes with sharp points. The lowest lobes are at 90 degrees to the leaf stem. Turn deep russet in late autumn. **FLOWERS** White and in loose clusters (corymbs), and 10–15mm across; five petals. **BARK** Pale grey, very closely scaled, flaking off to reveal dark patches. **BUDS** Bright green, like peas.

 Hermaphrodite, with male and female parts to each flower. **SEEDS** Single within fruits, dispersed by birds. **FLOWERS** Pollinated by insects. **LONGEVITY** To 300 years.

Fruits are edible, especially when well over (like dates).

ABOVE LEFT: *PALE GREY BARK, FLAKES EASILY*

ABOVE CENTRE: *SHARP-POINTED, LOBED LEAVES*

ABOVE RIGHT: *UNAPPETISING BROWN FRUITS*

BELOW LEFT: *WHITE FLOWERS IN RATHER OPEN CLUSTERS*

BELOW: *UNUSUAL GREEN BUDS*

⭐ The seeds have particularly strong seed cases, allowing them to be protected as the fruits pass through the guts of birds.

FACT FILE

FAMILY Rosaceae (Roses) HEIGHT Maximum 28m SIMILAR SPECIES Whitebeams and other shrubs. Quite distinctive.

JAN	FEB	MAR	APR	MAY	JUN	JUL	AUG	SEP	OCT	NOV	DEC

As a wild plant at forest edges and in open areas. Widely planted. Native.

SWEDISH WHITEBEAM

Sorbus intermedia

The Swedish Whitebeam is a medium-sized tree with a domed top, growing to 20m in height. It is native to the Baltic but has a special talent that, in recent years, has brought it to all parts of the region – the ability to cope with air pollution. As a result, it is widely planted along roads, and in car parks, public amenity sites, and many urban and suburban sites. It also spreads of its own accord, so is now a common tree.

 You can look no further than the fruits and leaves, although the bark, branches and flowers are also notable. **FRUITS** Berries (pomes), each 15mm long and 10mm across, are orange, which is highly unusual (see Sea Buckthorn, p. 138), but some are more scarlet. **LEAVES** Have the whitebeam signature of hairs on the undersides, making them greyish-white. Uppersides dark green. Leaves 12cm long and lobed, vaguely as in a Sessile Oak (p. 76), but they are quite shallow, and every lobe is spikily toothed. There are 6–9 pairs of veins. **BARK** Grey and relatively smooth. **BRANCHES** Often twist around. **FLOWERS** Grow in bunches (corymbs) of white blooms. Each flower has five petals. Similar to the Common Whitebeam (p. 104).

BELOW LEFT: *GREY , SMOOTH BARK*

BELOW CENTRE: *SHALLOWLY LOBED LEAVES*

BELOW RIGHT: *ORANGE BERRIES*

F A C T   F I L E

FAMILY Rosaceae (Roses) HEIGHT Maximum 20m SIMILAR SPECIES Other whitebeams.

ABOVE & RIGHT: *THE TREE IN WINTER AND SUMMER*

 Hermaphrodite, with male and female parts to each flower. **SEEDS** Two per fruit, dispersed by birds. **FLOWERS** Pollinated by insects. **LONGEVITY** Up to about 120 years.

 A popular ornamental.

The species is thought to have arisen as a cross between the Wild Service Tree (p. 106), Common Whitebeam and Rowan (p. 102).

BELOW: *GREEN BUDS*

JAN	FEB	MAR	APR	MAY	JUN	JUL	AUG	SEP	OCT	NOV	DEC

WILD PLUM

Prunus domestica

Gardens, waste places and hedges. Planted abundantly, and naturalizes easily. Originates from cultivation.

Wild Plums are a sweet conundrum. Their origin is not entirely certain, although they probably arose in cultivation as offspring of the Cherry Plum (opposite). In the wild they sow confusion by their fruits of many colours and tastes. Owing to a long history of crossbreeding, some are sweeter than others, some have frostier fruits and some bushes have spines – but they are all more or less the same thing, despite forms having different names, such as Greengage, Damson and Bullace. This is a small deciduous tree or large shrub, to 10m tall, with suckers.

BELOW: *FRUITS*

 Best known for its fruits, but also has heavenly flower blossom and quite distinctive leaves. **FRUITS** Plums, 2–7cm long, egg shaped and in a variety of luscious colours – black, purple, red, green and yellow. **FLOWERS** Slightly off-white, sometimes with a green tinge. Grow in loose clusters of 2–3 close to the stem, and each has five petals and is 15–25mm across. **LEAVES** Oval (usually broadest just beyond halfway) and have small teeth. On many plants, leaves are downy on the underside. Leaves 3–8cm long. **TWIGS** Grey-brown and in some plants spiny. Branches straight. **BARK** Purplish.

 Male and female parts in same flower. **SEEDS** Singly in fruits, dispersed by birds and mammals. **FLOWERS** Pollinated by insects. **LONGEVITY** Up to 20 years.

 Quite apart from being edible fresh, dried plums are known as prunes and have mild laxative properties.

 Plums are the world's second most cultivated fruit after tomatoes.

FACT FILE

FAMILY Rosaceae (Roses) HEIGHT Maximum 10m. SIMILAR SPECIES Cherry Plum (opposite), Blackthorn and Wild Cherry (pp. 112 and 114).

JAN	FEB	MAR	APR	MAY	JUN	JUL	AUG	SEP	OCT	NOV	DEC

CHERRY PLUM

Prunus cerasifera

The Cherry Plum might be completely overlooked among the many flowering fruit trees were it not for its amazingly early spring blossom – it is well under way by February and its leaves are not far behind, making it a firm favourite for beautifying streets. Introduced from south-east Europe, it is a small deciduous tree or large shrub, which suckers, usually growing to about 12m.

small tree, often in leaf very early

Commonly planted on streets and in hedges, and naturalized on waste ground and in parks. Introduced.

ABOVE: *MANY FORMS HAVE PURPLE LEAVES*

BELOW: *THE FIVE-PETALLED FLOWERS*

The early flowers are a clue to its identification, as well as its distinctive fruits. The leaves and shoots also merit checking. **FLOWERS** Bright white (whiter than those of the Blackthorn, p. 112) and emerge in February. They are comparatively large, 1–2cm across, each with five petals, and grow in small clusters. **FRUITS** Usually red or yellow. They are drupes, each 2–3cm across. **LEAVES** Pale glossy-green, slightly toothed, oval, and 3–7cm long. **SHOOTS** Glossy green (not black as in the Blackthorn) and do not usually have spines. **BARK** Dark grey to purplish.

Male and female parts are in the same flower. **SEEDS** Singly in berries, dispersed by birds and mammals. **FLOWERS** Pollinated by insects. **LONGEVITY** About 20 years.

Very much an ornamental tree, although the plums are used as a soup flavouring or as a local alcoholic tipple.

FACT FILE

FAMILY Rosaceae (Roses) HEIGHT Maximum 15m SIMILAR SPECIES Blackthorn and Wild Plum (opposite). Also known as the Myrobalan Plum.

JAN	FEB	MAR	APR	MAY	JUN	JUL	AUG	SEP	OCT	NOV	DEC

BLACKTHORN

Prunus spinosa

Open woods, hedgerows and scrub. Native and abundant.

It may or may not snow in winter, but where the Blackthorn grows, from late February the flowers of this shrub burst out and coat the landscape with a blaze of white. The sheer volume of this foamy blossom is a marvel, not just to the human eye, but also to hungry pollinators for whom the flowers are an essential early source of nectar. The Blackthorn's other gift is its fruit, which is beloved by birds and can also be used to make a tasty drink, sloe gin. The only downside to this wondrous shrub is its ferocious thorns. The Blackthorn is a spiny deciduous shrub, usually up to 4m in height. Its suckers form dense thickets.

BELOW LEFT: *NARROW, OVAL LEAVES*

BELOW CENTRE: *FLOWERS WITH YELLOW-TIPPED ANTHERS*

BELOW RIGHT: *EARLY SEASON FRUITS*

The flowers are so early and so voluminous that they are as easy to identify as Common Hazel catkins (p. 68). See also the fruits (berries), twigs, leaves and buds. **FLOWERS** Five-petalled, pristine white, growing along shoots, 1.5cm across. The yellow-tipped stamens are longer than the petals and are obvious. **FRUITS** 'Sloes' are drupes, 10–15mm in diameter. Globular, bluish-black, with a misty sheen. **TWIGS** Distinctively black, with the famous thorns forming from side shoots. **LEAVES** Unremarkable, oval, twice as long as broad (broadest

FACT FILE

FAMILY Rosaceae (Roses) HEIGHT Maximum 5m SIMILAR SPECIES Cherry Plum (p. 111).

ABOVE: *DARK SHOOTS AND STEMS*

early blossom can look like snow

above halfway), toothed and 2–4cm long. **BUDS** Often in clusters.

 Male and female parts occur in the same flower. **SEEDS** In berries, dispersed by birds and mammals. **FLOWERS** Pollinated by insects. **LONGEVITY** Up to 100 years.

LEFT & ABOVE: *THE TREE IN SUMMER AND SPRING*

BELOW: *BUDS IN CLUSTERS*

 Berries are edible if very bitter, and can be used to infuse gin and vodka. The thorny nature of the Blackthorn makes it ideal for hedges and borders.

 The wood is very strong and, when Blackthorn scrub is being cleared, it sometimes punctures tractor tyres.

 Known for forming impenetrable, fiercely thorny thickets.

JAN	FEB	MAR	APR	MAY	JUN	JUL	AUG	SEP	OCT	NOV	DEC

WILD CHERRY

Prunus avium

Cherries are the classic blossom trees, and there are multiple types in cultivation. In the wild, however, if you see white fulsome blossom in the treetops, it is usually this species. The blossom does not last long, and a brisk wind will make a 'snowstorm' out of the petals, which soon carpet the ground. The Wild Cherry needs lots of light to thrive, so is usually found on the fringes of woods and in hedgerows. It is a popular tree, planted widely. The fruits, smaller than those of cultivated cherries, are a much-loved summer snack for birds. The Wild Cherry is a small to medium-sized deciduous tree, to 25m tall, forming suckers.

Woodland edges and hedgerows. Native and common.

BELOW: *REDDISH BUDS IN CLUSTERS*

 Readily identified by its flowers, fruits and bark. **FLOWERS** The early spring blossom comes out just before the leaves. Flowers are in long-stalked bunches of 2–6, each as crisp white as clean sheets. They have five broad petals, and are each 15–30mm in diameter. **FRUITS** Small versions of cultivated cherries, in the same familiar long-stalked bunches. They are drupes up to 2cm in diameter, and red to dark red in colour. **BARK** Unusual for its reddish-brown hue, with horizontal peeled sections and almost orange scars. **LEAVES** Quite large, 6–15cm long, on

can be a relatively substantial tree

ABOVE & LEFT: *THE TREE IN WINTER AND SUMMER*

long stalks. They are oval, with sharp points, and with significant teeth giving a serrated edge. Look out for the red glands at the base of each leaf, at the top of the stalk (see Star Facts, below). Turn orange and red in autumn. **BUDS** In clusters on the flowering twigs, a rich reddish colour, and oval.

ABOVE LEFT: REDDISH-BROWN BARK WITH HORIZONTAL PEELINGS

ABOVE CENTRE: LEAVES WITH SERRATED EDGES ON LONG STALKS

ABOVE RIGHT: FLOWERS ARE WHITE CUPS

 Flowers contain male and female parts. **SEEDS** The stones of the cherries, bird and mammal dispersed. **FLOWERS** Pollinated by insects, especially bees. **LONGEVITY** About 60 years.

Timber a rich reddish-brown, almost like mahogany.

The red glands at the base of the leaf produce nectar, attracting insects such as ants that attack other insects, thus protecting the leaf.

RIGHT: *RED GLANDS AT BASE OF LEAF*

F A C T   F I L E

FAMILY Rosaceae (Roses) HEIGHT Maximum 32m SIMILAR SPECIES Cherry Plum, Bird Cherry (pp. 111 and 116), and Plum *P. domestica*. Also known as the European Cherry.

JAN	FEB	MAR	APR	MAY	JUN	JUL	AUG	SEP	OCT	NOV	DEC

Woodland and scrub. Native. Northern (to Arctic Circle).

BELOW: *WHITE FLOWER SPIKE*

BIRD CHERRY

Prunus padus

You have to be quick to get the best of this tree. The spikes of blossom are fantastic in late spring, but soon disappear. In Sweden and Finland the flowering of the Bird Cherry is revered as the start of summer. Then, as is typical of cherries, the fruits arrive in July, and are consumed by the local birds – being small and easily swallowed – within a few days. Some befall complete defoliation by a small moth, the Bird Cherry Ermine, which leaves a skeletal shrub covered in silk. The Bird Cherry is a deciduous tree or shrub usually to 15m tall; it produces suckers.

The flowers are easy to recognize and the buds are unusual. Also note the fruits, leaves and bark. **FLOWERS** White and in elongated spikes (racemes) with 10–40 flowers, giving a well-endowed shrub. Flowers are 10–15mm long, and the spike can be 15cm long – quite unlike the Wild Cherry flowers (p. 114). Flowers sweetly scented, reminding some people of almonds **BUDS** Sharply pointed and not in clusters like those of the Wild Cherry. They run alongside the shoots. **FRUITS** Small black, shiny, spherical cherries, 6–8mm across. They are bitter. **LEAVES** Dull green, oval, with a small tip, almost invisibly but many toothed, 5–10cm long. **BARK** Dull greyish-black, smelling unpleasant if rubbed.

late-spring blossom

Male and female parts are within the same flower. **SEEDS** The cherry stones, dispersed by birds and mammals, which consume the fruits. **FLOWERS** Insect pollinated. **LONGEVITY** 20–50 years.

Popular ornamental tree.

FACT FILE

FAMILY Rosaceae (Roses) HEIGHT Maximum 19m SIMILAR SPECIES Other cherries.

JAN	FEB	MAR	APR	MAY	JUN	JUL	AUG	SEP	OCT	NOV	DEC

CHERRY LAUREL

Prunus laurocerasus

understory shrub

This tall, sprawling evergreen shrub usually grows to 8m tall and makes a good hedge, but it tends to have loftier aspirations, often self-seeding and growing from suckers to create, if unchecked, something of a monster. It is shade, dry-weather and cold tolerant, so is something of a super-shrub. Its flowers are glorious in spring.

Woods, scrub and gardens. Introduced from south-east Europe and south-west Asia.

ABOVE: *LARGE WAXY LEAVES*

BELOW: *FLOWER SPIKES*

Identified by its evergreen leaves, and by its flowers and fruits. **LEAVES** Glossy evergreen, very big, up to 20cm long and 6cm broad, with a blunt tip. **FLOWERS** In spikes of up to 30 flowers, covering the shrub in spring. They are erect, with each flower being up to 7–9mm across, and each spike to 13cm long. Individual flowers white. **FRUITS** Shiny black and look poisonous but are perfectly edible, 10–15mm across. **TWIGS** Green.

Male and female parts are within the same flower. **SEEDS** Cherry stones, dispersed by birds and mammals, which consume the fruits. **FLOWERS** Insect pollinated. **LONGEVITY** 40 years.

Used as cover for game and as hedging.

The leaves and seeds contain hydrogen cyanide.

FACT FILE

FAMILY Rosaceae (Roses) HEIGHT Maximum 10m SIMILAR SPECIES The similar Portugal Laurel *P. lusitanica* has thinner leaves with sharper tips.

JAN	FEB	MAR	APR	MAY	JUN	JUL	AUG	SEP	OCT	NOV	DEC

FIELD MAPLE

Acer campestre

Woodland and hedges, on chalk or clay soils. Native and common.

This is a deciduous small, neat, almost petite tree or shrub with a dense network of branches on a thick trunk. It usually grows to 20m tall and is often rounded on top with dense branches. Equally, the small, ivy-like leaves are also dense, and this means that in autumn, when they turn a glorious golden-yellow, it makes for a very impressive sight. Although a remarkable tree in its own right, it is often found as no more than a bush, either on the margins of woods or, more usually, as a coppice in hedges.

 Distinctive leaves, fruits and flowers. Also note the bark and twigs. **LEAVES** Five lobed, with blunt tips, and opposite. They are small and, when fresh, often slightly reddish. Much smaller and blunter than those of the Sycamore (p. 122) or Norway Maple (p. 120), 3–5cm long (Sycamore and Norway Maple leaves to 15cm long). If you break a leaf stalk, it exudes a milky sap (no sap in Sycamore, but same as Norway Maple). **FRUITS** Paired, winged achenes, in bunches of four. Each achene about 3cm long. Wings opposite each other at an angle of 180 degrees (see Sycamore). Note fresh red-and-green colour. **FLOWERS** In yellowish-green clusters. They point upwards, rather than hanging as in the Sycamore. There are usually fewer flowers (10

ABOVE: *SMALL, REDDISH-BROWN BUDS*

BELOW, LEFT TO RIGHT: *ERECT FLOWER CLUSTERS; BLUNT-TIPPED LEAVES*

FACT FILE

FAMILY Sapindaceae (Maples) HEIGHT Maximum 26m SIMILAR SPECIES Norway Maple and Sycamore, see following pages.

BELOW: *LIGHT BROWN TRUNK*

densely-packed tree, often at woodland edge

ABOVE & LEFT: *THE TREE IN SUMMER AND WINTER*

as opposed to about 30 or more). Each flower 6mm across, with five petals. **BARK** Bright brown with a wonderful network of vertical fissures and bosses. **TWIGS** Downy at first and develop 'wings' and stripy wrinkles, giving a corky look. **BUDS** Small, reddish-brown, opposite.

Flowers usually physically both male and female, but often only function as one gender per plant. Insect pollinated. **SEEDS** Spread by the wind (see above), in twos, helicoptering downwards. **LONGEVITY** Up to 350 years.

Wood often used for making musical instruments, notably harps.

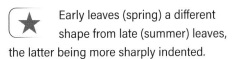

Early leaves (spring) a different shape from late (summer) leaves, the latter being more sharply indented.

BELOW: *DISTINCTIVE WINGED SEEDS, OFTEN WITH PINK EDGES*

JAN	FEB	MAR	APR	MAY	JUN	JUL	AUG	SEP	OCT	NOV	DEC

Woodland, hedges and rough grassland. Native to Europe but not Britain. Common.

BELOW: *GREY, NEATLY FISSURED BARK*

NORWAY MAPLE

Acer platanoides

You can almost imagine, in the quest to be fashionably spiky, that the Norway Maple wanted to outdo the blunt-lobed Field Maple (p. 118) and the fairly angular Sycamore (p. 122), so evolved leaves that are bigger and sharper. Overall, the leaves are less madly packed in than a Field Maple, giving this tree a more open crown. Although abundant on the Continent, the Norway Maple is naturally absent from Britain, although widely planted. Despite its English name, it is only native to a small part of Norway. This is a medium-sized deciduous tree to 30m tall, with a rounded crown.

 Best identified by its leaves. The flowers are also distinctive, and the fruits are the familiar winged 'samaras' of maples. **LEAVES** Five lobed and each lobe has several sharp teeth, distinct from the leaves of the Field Maple and Sycamore. When snapped, the leaf stem exudes milky sap (not Sycamore). The leaves turn yellow in autumn. Leaves opposite, and 7–14cm long and across. **FRUITS** Paired, winged samaras of maples. The wings are at a wide angle, approaching 180 degrees to each other (as in the Field Maple, but those of the Sycamore are angled at 90 degrees). Wings 3–5cm long. **FLOWERS** In clusters of 15–30,

ABOVE: *BROAD, REDDISH-BROWN BUDS*

ABOVE LEFT: *DISTINCTIVE, SPIKY LEAVES*

ABOVE RIGHT: *FLOWERS NOT TIGHTLY CLUSTERED*

erect like those of the Field Maple (hanging in Sycamore). They are yellow like those of the Field Maple, but less packed. **BARK** Distinctly greyer than that of the Field Maple, without any warm tones. It is neatly fissured and does not age visibly. **BUDS** Fairly broad and shiny reddish-brown.

 Flowers contain male and female parts, but an individual tree may only be functionally of one gender. **SEEDS** Flattened, each within a winged fruit known as a samara. **LONGEVITY** Up to 250 years in the wild, but usually much less.

BELOW: *FRUITS ALMOST AT 180 DEGREES*

 The wood is strong and pale, and is ideal for furniture making.

Leaves begin to fall in autumn when the daylight drops to below 10 hours.

FACT FILE

FAMILY Sapindaceae (Maples) HEIGHT Maximum 30m
SIMILAR SPECIES Field Maple and Sycamore.

JAN	FEB	MAR	APR	MAY	JUN	JUL	AUG	SEP	OCT	NOV	DEC

SYCAMORE

Acer pseudoplatanus

The Sycamore, a large, domed, broad deciduous tree generally to about 30m tall, is something of a superhero among trees, with a number of exceptional attributes. Almost alone, it can cope with violent winds and salt spray on exposed northern headlands, while it also grows very fast and spreads extremely efficiently with its winged seeds. It casts a deep shade to prevent the growth of other plants, and also poisons the soil when its leaves fall. It is abundant, often dominant and seemingly unstoppable. Amazingly, its natural range in Europe only originally reached northern France, but it has been in Britain since 1500 and seems thoroughly at home in colder climates.

Easiest to identify by its winged fruits but also note its flowers and leaves. **FRUITS** The samaras are double and winged, hanging in clusters called keys. The aerodynamic properties of the wings ensure that they twirl down rather than drop, helicoptering further away from the parent tree. The angle of the two wings is about 90 degrees (see maples, pp. 118–121). **LEAVES** Large for size of tree (7–16cm long) and divided into five lobes, each lobe with irregular and rather blunt teeth. Leaves are in opposite pairs. They are dark green and a rather disappointing wan yellow in autumn, just dropping without

Almost any soil and any habitat except acid bogs and moorland.

ABOVE: *GREEN BUDS IN OPPOSITE PAIRS*

BELOW, LEFT TO RIGHT:
*FIVE-LOBED LEAVES;
FRUITS AT 90 DEGREES*

FACT FILE

FAMILY Sapindaceae (Maples) HEIGHT Maximum 38m SIMILAR SPECIES Maples.

BELOW & RIGHT: *THE TREE IN WINTER AND SUMMER*

domed at top

ceremony. They often have dark blotches. Young leaves do not exude milky sap (see maples). **FLOWERS** In hanging clusters called panicles, like broad pipe cleaners. The 100 or so flowers are yellow-green. Flower spikes 5–20cm long. **BARK** Greyish-pink and flaky (smooth when young). **BUDS** Large, green and in opposite pairs. Hairless.

 Flowers usually physically both male and female, but often only function as one gender per plant. **SEEDS** Spread by the wind (see above), in twos. **LONGEVITY** To about 400 years.

 The wood is often used to make spoons and other kitchenware.

 Sycamores attract many aphids, which exude copious amounts of honeydew, making the leaves sticky.

ABOVE: *GREYISH-PINK, FLAKY BARK*

JAN	FEB	MAR	APR	MAY	JUN	JUL	AUG	SEP	OCT	NOV	DEC

Usually in parks and streets, on rough ground. Introduced to the area from the Balkans. Common.

HORSE CHESTNUT

Aesculus hippocastanum

Is there a kinder tree than the Horse Chestnut to those who wish to learn tree identification? Its leaves, flowers and fruits are all really easy to identify. It is much loved for producing its large seeds, conkers, in autumn, and these are shiny and shapely, making them perfect for autumn decoration and for the game in which children attempt to break one another's conker at the end of a string. Despite the tree's familiarity and popularity, it is only native to a small area of the Balkans east to Turkmenistan. This is a large deciduous tree, often domed, usually growing to 25m tall.

Easy – often planted in readily accessible places such as parks, so is well known and familiar. **LEAVES** Hand-sized leaves divided into leaflets (usually seven). Leaflets up to 30cm long. Horse Chestnuts are the only plants with opposite palmate leaves. Very few trees in the area have leaves divided this way. They easily rust in late

overall domed shape

ABOVE & LEFT: *THE TREE IN WINTER AND SUMMER*

summer. **FLOWERS** Wondrous erect 'candles' of opulent white flowers. Bases yellow but turn red after pollination. Spires can be 15–30cm tall. **FRUITS** Nuts 5–8cm long, fleshy green and spiny, looking like some sea creature out of water. **BUDS** Large, red-brown and sticky. **TRUNK** Grey and flaky.

 Male and female occur in the same flower. **SEEDS** 'Conkers', usually one in each capsule. **FLOWERS** Insect pollinated. **LONGEVITY** Up to 300 years.

 The game of conkers can be ideal for children to learn about competitiveness and pain.

ABOVE LEFT: GREY, FLAKY BARK

ABOVE CENTRE: DIVIDED LEAVES OFTEN STAINED IN LATE SUMMER BY THE HORSE CHESTNUT LEAF MINER MOTH

ABOVE RIGHT: IMPRESSIVE FLOWER SPIKES

BELOW: LARGE STICKY BUDS

★ When a leaf falls, it leaves a scar in a remarkably horseshoe-like shape.

LEFT: THE FAMOUS SEEDS OR 'CONKERS'

FACT FILE

FAMILY Sapindaceae (Maples) **HEIGHT** Maximum 39m **SIMILAR SPECIES** None, but the similarly named Sweet Chestnut (p. 72) is also a big tree with conspicuous seeds.

JAN	FEB	MAR	APR	MAY	JUN	JUL	AUG	SEP	OCT	NOV	DEC

COMMON LABURNUM

Laburnum anagyroides

Gardens, hedges, waste ground and scrub; often self-sown. Introduced from southern Europe.

Few shrubs are as ludicrously adorned as the extraordinary Common Laburnum, with its fountains of hanging, brilliant yellow flowers. Not surprisingly, it is a garden favourite, providing midsummer joy. Like every beauty, however, it has a dark side, in this case being thoroughly poisonous. It is a small deciduous tree reaching 8m in height.

Instantly recognizable by the flowers. Also note the leaves, bark and fruits. **FLOWERS** Yellow, in long, hanging clusters known as racemes, 15–30cm long. Each flower has five petals, two above and three below, like many flowers in the pea family, and is 2cm long. **LEAVES** In threes at the end of a shared stalk (a little like clover).

BELOW RIGHT: *THE UNMISTAKEABLE FLOWER CLUSTERS*

They are 2–3cm long. **BARK** Distinctively greenish and smooth. **FRUITS** Brown hanging pods 4–6cm long, 1–3 from each flower cluster.

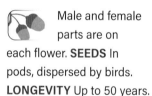

Male and female parts are on each flower. **SEEDS** In pods, dispersed by birds. **LONGEVITY** Up to 50 years.

fabulous fountains of blossom

FACT FILE

FAMILY Fabaceae/Leguminosae (Peas) HEIGHT Maximum 8m SIMILAR SPECIES Other members of the pea family have yellow blooms, such as Gorse *Ulex europaeus* and brooms *Cytisus* spp.

JAN	FEB	MAR	APR	MAY	JUN	JUL	AUG	SEP	OCT	NOV	DEC

RHODODENDRON

Rhododendron ponticum

abundant purple flowers

Woodland, woodland edges and open areas, such as hillsides, on acid soils. Introduced from south-west Europe. Very common.

ABOVE: *NEAT BUD*

BELOW: *LONG, NARROW, EVERGREEN LEAVES*

Liked by some gardeners and walkers in woods and parks, Rhododendrons are unpopular with conservationists. They are all but useless for wildlife and have a nasty habit of spreading by suckers from the roots and taking over large patches of woodland or hillside; they can be a nightmare to control. The plant harbours a fungus that kills oak and larch trees, and it shades out native flora. It is also mildly toxic to the touch. It is an evergreen, with suckering shrubs, to 5m tall.

The wonderful flowers make it famous, but check also the leaves, fruits and twigs. **FLOWERS** In crowded clusters of 10–15, usually purple or pink, funnel-shaped blooms, each 4–6cm in diameter, and with five petals and long anthers. **LEAVES** Big (8–20cm long, 2–5cm wide), leathery and evergreen, each on a very hairy stalk. They are long and narrow with a pointed tip. **FRUITS** 1.5–2.5cm-long dry capsules. **BARK** Reddish.

Each flower contains male and female parts. **SEEDS** In large numbers within fruit capsules. **FLOWERS** Insect pollinated. **LONGEVITY** 60–80 years.

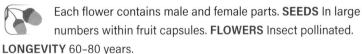

FACT FILE

FAMILY Ericaceae (Rhododendrons) HEIGHT Maximum 5m
SIMILAR SPECIES Cherry Laurel (p. 117).

JAN	FEB	MAR	APR	MAY	JUN	JUL	AUG	SEP	OCT	NOV	DEC

HOLLY

Ilex aquifolium

Woodland, scrub, hedges and moors, sometimes making its own woods. Native. Common on well-drained soils.

One of the easiest of all trees to identify, the Holly is an evergreen shrub or small tree, usually to 10m tall. It is renowned for its shiny green, prickly foliage and festive red berries, welcome colour in the dark canvas of midwinter, especially around Christmas time. It is kind to birds, too, the berries being a welcome source of winter food, although they are toxic to humans. It is a common understorey tree in many woods, and also occurs in the open on various soils, sometimes even building its own, very atmospheric form of woodland. The extreme density and prickliness of the foliage makes it a superb hideout for many forms of wildlife.

Usually instantly identified by its leaves and often detected by its fruits. Also note the bark and flowers. **LEAVES** You cannot look beyond these, since they are unique, with their spiny margins. Note that leaves above grazing range may not be spiny, and some individuals are all but spineless, but they are always hard and glossy above. They grow alternately on the stem, and are each 3–12cm long. Some cultivated forms of Holly have pale blotches on the leaves or complete pale edges (variegated). **FRUITS** Familiar crimson-red berries, 6–10cm across, in clusters. **BARK** Smooth and grey, with ridges

BELOW LEFT: *FAMOUS PRICKLY LEAVES*

BELOW RIGHT: WHITE *FLOWERS*

FACT FILE

FAMILY Aquifoliaceae (Hollies) HEIGHT Maximum 23m SIMILAR SPECIES Evergreen Oak and Bay (pp. 78 and 87).

BELOW: *BRIGHT RED BERRIES*

and multiple round warts. Shoots green. **FLOWERS** White, in clusters at bases of leaves. They each have four petals and are 5–7mm across. Male flowers are fragrant.

 Males and females are on different plants (in fact they all bear non-functioning parts of one sex or the other). **SEEDS** Dispersed by birds and mammals. **FLOWERS** Insect pollinated. **LONGEVITY** Up to 300 years.

 The wood is often used for walking sticks.

 A Holly leaf lasts about seven years.

 The leaf is spined to protect it from browsing deer, but the outer edge is thickened to deter caterpillars, which tend to start feeding on a leaf from the edge.

ABOVE: *SMOOTH GREY BARK*

JAN	FEB	MAR	APR	MAY	JUN	JUL	AUG	SEP	OCT	NOV	DEC

SPINDLE

Euonymus europaeus

The Spindle would probably be a largely overlooked shrub were it not for its extraordinary fruits, which are unique. Shocking coral-pink and orange, they look so tacky and false in the bare winter landscape that they could be Christmas decorations left behind for the January sales. The garish colour attracts birds, which eat the orange aril flesh and excrete the poisonous seeds. The Spindle is named for its wood, which was once used for spindles employed in wool spinning. It is a deciduous, much-branched shrub usually to 6m tall.

Woodland edges, scrub and hedgerows, almost always on chalk and other lime-rich soils. Native, fairly common and southern.

Easy in autumn only. Other than the fruits, look out for the unusual green shoots (twigs) and colourful bark. The flowers are easy to miss. **FRUITS** Once seen, never forgotten, the hanging fruits consist of four pink capsules, which split to reveal bright orange arils (seed coverings), 8–15mm across. **SHOOTS** Straight, four sided and remain green for three years, which can draw attention to this species in late winter. **BARK** Olive-green with

low, multi-branched shrub

ABOVE: *BARK WITH TAWNY STREAKS*

unusual tawny-coloured ripples. **FLOWERS** Dull greenish-yellow, as if embarrassed by the opulent seeds. They are four petalled, in a crucifix shape, and 8–20cm across. **LEAVES** Unexciting in summer, just oval, point tipped with very small teeth, and about 8cm long. However, they turn a gorgeous red in autumn. **BUDS** Green, set flat against the stem.

Male and female occur on the same flower. **SEEDS** Four, with orange surface, dispersed by birds. **FLOWERS** Insect pollinated (usually by flies). **LONGEVITY** More than 100 years.

The hard wood has been used for toothpicks and knitting needles. The fruits were once baked and rubbed into the hair to get rid of lice.

Up to 17 per cent of all the tree's annual sugar production comes from the bark not the leaves.

ABOVE LEFT: *POINTED OVAL LEAVES*

ABOVE RIGHT: *SMALL, GREENISH-WHITE FLOWERS*

BELOW: *THE ASTONISHING FRUITS*

FACT FILE

FAMILY Celastraceae (Spindles) HEIGHT Maximum 9m SIMILAR SPECIES Dogwood (p. 132).

| JAN | FEB | MAR | APR | MAY | JUN | JUL | AUG | SEP | OCT | NOV | DEC |

DOGWOOD

Cornus sanguinea

Woodland edges and hedges, especially on chalk and limestone but also clays. Native and common. Southern.

The Dogwood is unique among Britain's shrubs in having instantly recognizable twigs. The scarlet colour of the first-year shoots adds a welcome dash of brightness to the gloomy drudgery of midwinter, while the autumn foliage, a rich burgundy colour, is often stunning and is one of the first on any tree to turn in early autumn. This shrub is especially common on chalk downland, but various types are planted in gardens and parks for winter colour.

Unusual for its colourful twigs. Note the unique leaf quirk (see below). The white flowers are easy to recognize and so are the blackish berries and winter buds. The red-stained first-year twigs are unmistakable. **LEAVES** Note that you can pull the leaves apart gently from each end and they will split, leaving several 'strings' of elastic tissue joining the two pieces. No other leaves do this. The leaves have very pronounced veins that do not orientate straight to the end, but curve towards the tip. They are a pleasing oval shape, without teeth, and 4–8cm long and about 3cm wide. (See the Spindle, p. 130.) They turn early (September). **FLOWERS** The flat-topped flowerheads contain clusters of small, creamy flowers, with four stamens and one

BELOW LEFT: *LEAF VEINS CURVE TOWARDS TIP*

BELOW CENTRE: *STAR-LIKE FLOWER CLUSTERS*

BELOW RIGHT: *GRAPE-LIKE BERRIES*

FACT FILE

FAMILY Cornaceae (Dogwoods) HEIGHT Can reach 10m SIMILAR SPECIES The Spindle has similar flowers; the berries resemble those of buckthorns (pp. 135–139) and Wild Privet (p. 148).

style, each 4–7mm across, of a satisfyingly neat, geometric cross-shape. (See Spindle with green flowers.) **FRUITS** Black berries (drupes), 5–8mm across, in grape-like clusters on the red shoots. **BUDS** Reddish, bristly and without scales. Opposite.

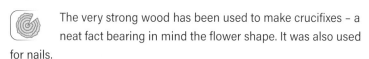 Male and female occur within the same flower. **SEEDS** Red, 1–2 in each berry, dispersed by birds. **FRUITS** Berries eaten and seeds spread by birds. **FLOWERS** Insect pollinated. **LONGEVITY** 80 years.

The very strong wood has been used to make crucifixes – a neat fact bearing in mind the flower shape. It was also used for nails.

Arrows found beside the famous 'Ice Man' mummy discovered in the Alps in 1991 were made of Dogwood.

ABOVE: *GREY-BROWN AND RATHER NEATLY FISSURED BARK*

LEFT: *REDDISH BUDS*

JAN	FEB	MAR	APR	MAY	JUN	JUL	AUG	SEP	OCT	NOV	DEC

BOX

Buxus sempervirens

Wild Box is not common in the area, preferring warm places on chalk, and is much more at home in the Mediterranean. However, it is a plant we all know, because the tiny, thick, evergreen leaves are perfect for hedges, and are used everywhere. They respond with equanimity to being cut into shapes – no matter that the leaves smell like the urine of a tomcat. The Box is a dense evergreen shrub, usually to 5m tall.

Woods and scrub, mainly on chalk and limestone. Native, but far more likely to be seen everywhere as a garden hedge.

The leaves stand out, as does the dense shape. Also note the twigs, flowers and bark. **LEAVES** Evergreen and small, only 1–2.5cm long. They are shiny, rounded and leathery, unlike anything else. Each leaf lies opposite a pair on the stem. **TWIGS** Green and four sided. **FLOWERS** Scented flowers tiny (1mm long), greenish and without petals; in small clusters at the base of the leaves. Single female flower surrounded by 5–6 male flowers. **FRUITS** Green three-lobed capsule, 8mm long. **BARK** Tightly ridged, grey with traces of pale brown.

Male and female flowers found on the same plant. **SEEDS** 3–6 in each fruit capsule, dispersed when capsule splits open. **FLOWERS** Insect pollinated, scented. **LONGEVITY** 20–30 years.

dense bush

ABOVE: *TINY WHITE FLOWERS AND LEATHERY LEAVES*

FACT FILE

FAMILY Buxaceae (Boxes) HEIGHT Maximum 12m SIMILAR SPECIES Bay (p. 87).

JAN	FEB	MAR	APR	MAY	JUN	JUL	AUG	SEP	OCT	NOV	DEC

ALDER BUCKTHORN

Frangula alnus

A low-growing, spreading deciduous shrub (sometimes a small tree), the Alder Buckthorn is easy to miss but for its berries in summer, which are often of different colours. It is most unusual in having yellow bark, which you can discover by stripping back the outer layer of twigs. The name Alder Buckthorn refers to the leaves, which are quite similar to those of the Common Alder (p. 64), often growing nearby.

Damp woodland, bogs and scrub, especially on acidic soils. Native and localized.

LEFT: *LEAF VEINS DON'T REACH THE EDGE*

The fruits are easiest to pick out, but the leaves and flowers are important. Also check the buds when present. **FRUITS** Berries 6–10mm across, often having several colours at once (see the Wayfaring Tree, p. 156). They start green, then go yellow, red and finally black by early autumn. **LEAVES** Broad and oval, 2–7cm long, with the 6–10 veins looping around to meet at the tip (see also Purging Buckthorn, p. 136, and Dogwood, p. 132). They are not toothed, unlike those of the Purging Buckthorn, and generally alternate along the stem. **FLOWERS** Tiny, just 3–5mm across, white and star-like in dense clusters at the bases of the leaves. They have five petals (the Purging Buckthorn has four). **BUDS** Hairy, without scales (and alternate). **TWIGS** Often knobbly and go off in all directions.

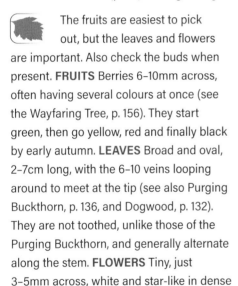

low-growing, easily overlooked

Male and female flowers are on different plants, although flowers retain vestigial parts of both sexes. **SEEDS** 2–3 within each berry, spread by birds. **LONGEVITY** 15–20 years.

ABOVE: *LATE AUTUMN BERRIES*

FACT FILE

FAMILY Rhamnaceae (Buckthorns) HEIGHT Maximum 7m SIMILAR SPECIES Purging Buckthorn and Dogwood.

JAN	FEB	MAR	APR	MAY	JUN	JUL	AUG	SEP	OCT	NOV	DEC

PURGING BUCKTHORN

Rhamnus cathartica

Open woodland, scrub, hedges and sometimes fens. Native and fairly common, especially on chalk and lime.

The low profile of this dense, spiny deciduous shrub or small tree, usually to 6m tall, can be summed up by the fact that it is probably best known as the food plant for one of Britain's favourite butterflies, the Brimstone – find the insect and you will find the plant, and vice versa. Having said that, if you were ever unfortunate or foolish enough to try the berries, you would undoubtedly remember the plant forever. Their legendary laxative properties were summed up by a certain Henry Lyte, who wrote in 1578 that 'they do purge downward mightily ... with great force and violence and excesse'.

BELOW LEFT: *STRAIGHT, THORNY TWIGS*

BELOW CENTRE: *FLOWERS, FOUR-PETALLED AND GREEN*

BELOW RIGHT: *GREEN BERRIES TURN BLACK LATER*

Notable for the twigs with spines, and also note the leaves, fruits and flowers. **TWIGS** Straight and untidy, and thorny (unlike Alder Buckthorn, p. 135). If you peel back the bark, the wood is orange (yellow in the Alder Buckthorn). **LEAVES** Broad and pointed, with teeth; 3–9cm long. The main veins loop around, meeting at the leaf tip as in the Dogwood (p. 132), but that plant's leaves lack teeth. There are 2–5 vein pairs (6–10 in the Alder Buckthorn, which also lacks teeth). Turn yellow in autumn. **FRUITS** Black berries (drupes) 6–10mm

FACT FILE

FAMILY Rhamnaceae (Buckthorns) HEIGHT Maximum 8m SIMILAR SPECIES Alder Buckthorn and Dogwood.

often untidy looking

across. They start green and progress to black. **FLOWERS** Dull green and very small (just 3–5mm across) each with four petals. They cluster at the bases of leaves. **BARK** Dark brown, often with orange patches. **BUDS** Have scales, unlike in the Alder Buckthorn.

 Male and female flowers are on different plants, although flowers retain vestigial parts of both sexes. **SEEDS** 2–4 within each berry, spread by birds. **FLOWERS** Insect pollinated. **LONGEVITY** 15–20 years.

 The bark was once used to produce a yellow dye.

An invasive plant in North America.

JAN	FEB	MAR	APR	MAY	JUN	JUL	AUG	SEP	OCT	NOV	DEC

SEA BUCKTHORN

Hippophae rhamnoides

A medium-sized, sprawling shrub or small tree 1–8m tall, the Sea Buckthorn is most at home on coastal sand dunes and scrubby cliffs. Here this shrub can gain a rapid foothold, quickly covering large areas with its thorny twigs, which can at times swamp precious dune systems. However, the Sea Buckthorn has become a popular crop plant, harvested for its vitamin C-rich berries.

Coastal dunes, sandy soil.

RIGHT: *GREY BARK WITH IRREGULAR RIDGES*

A low, sprawling, thorny blanket on dunes and coastal hillsides. The yellow-orange berries in autumn are unmistakable, as are the small, pale, clustered flower buds in spring. **FRUITS** Large clusters of

often forms dense thickets on dunes

yellow-orange berries packed along the stems of female shrubs in autumn. These nutrient-rich berries are eaten by overwintering birds and, though sour, are edible to humans. They endure over winter. **LEAVES** Lanceolate and round ended, growing alternately. Up to 4cm long, rather like long, soft pine needles. Silvery in colour and velvety to the touch. **FLOWERS** Small, abundant clusters of green, scaly inflorescences. **BARK** Rugged, brownish-grey with irregular ridges. **BUDS** Small and pale or shiny brown; knobbly, arranged in whorls along the grey stem, differing slightly in shape between male and female.

ABOVE LEFT: *LONG, SILVERY LEAVES*

ABOVE RIGHT: *DENSE CLUSTERS OF BERRIES*

 Dioecious – male and female trees both required for production of berries. Pollination by wind dispersal. **SEEDS** dispersed by animals – usually birds (see above). Also spreads by suckers. **LONGEVITY** 30 years or more.

BELOW: *WHORLS OF BUDS*

The leaves, seeds and berry flesh have been used for medicinal purposes for centuries; berries are now popular for making into jellies, syrups and juices.

Its scientific name means 'shiny horse', apparently on account of it traditionally being fed to horses to keep their coats glossy.

FACT FILE

FAMILY Elaeagnaceae (Oleasters) HEIGHT Maximum 8m SIMILAR SPECIES None.

JAN	FEB	MAR	APR	MAY	JUN	JUL	AUG	SEP	OCT	NOV	DEC

Woodlands on rich soils. Native. Frequently planted.

ABOVE: *REDDISH HAIRS AT BASE OF LEAF*

BELOW LEFT: *ROUNDED, HEART-SHAPED LEAVES*

BELOW RIGHT: *FLOWER CLUSTERS POINT UPWARDS*

SMALL-LEAVED LIME

Tilia cordata

This large, spreading, suckering deciduous tree, usually to 30m tall, can be quite a difficult tree to find. It is often hidden away in diverse mixed deciduous woodland, and in the region, is fairly localized and fussy, often thriving best on chalk and limestone. In Britain it is regarded as an indicator of ancient woodland (woodland in place for 400 plus years.) In midsummer, the fabulous rich, fragrant flowers – which do not look spectacular – are a magnet for a greater variety of insects than almost any other tree. The species is easily confused with other lime trees.

 Identified by the leaves, flowers, fruits, twigs and buds. **LEAVES** Heart shaped, sharply toothed and bulge more on one side than the other, as is the case with all limes. The leaves are very rounded, more so than in the Common Lime (p. 142). They are smaller (3–6cm long) than those of the Large-leaved Lime (p. 144) or Common Lime (6–12cm v 6–9cm long). Look for the tuft of reddish hairs on the veins at the base of the leaf (not on other limes). Otherwise greyish beneath. **FLOWERS** In small (4–10) clusters of five-petalled, wan yellow flowers with stamens as long as petals, which look like hairs sticking out. The cluster's stalk joins partway down a large, leaf-like bract, which

FACT FILE

FAMILY Malvaceae (Mallows) HEIGHT Maximum 40m SIMILAR SPECIES Large-leaved and Common Limes.

looks like a tongue. In this species the clusters point upwards from the bract; they do not hang. **FRUITS** Small round nuts (drupes), 6–7mm long. They fall in autumn, still attached to the bract, which propels them. **TWIGS** Distinctive in winter, zigzagging and bright red. In this species they are hairless (hairy only in the Large-leaved Lime, p. 144). **BUDS** Plump and look like 'boxing gloves', with one big and one small scale. They are 4–7mm across. **BARK** Smooth and grey, often breaking away in flakes, with many bosses. Branches sinuous.

 Male and female parts are on the same flower. **SEEDS** 1–2 per nut. **LONGEVITY** Some ancient, coppiced specimens are supposedly 6,000 years old.

 Nectar-rich leaves provide food for bees, which produce an exceptional honey.

 Between 6,000 and 5,000 years ago, the Small-leaved Lime was the most common tree in Britain, dominating many woods.

BELOW: *PLUMP BUDS*

JAN	FEB	MAR	APR	MAY	JUN	JUL	AUG	SEP	OCT	NOV	DEC

Rare in the wild, but abundantly planted everywhere, including along streets.

COMMON LIME

Tilia x *europaea*

Do not park your car under a lime in summer. The trees are such a magnet for aphids and other insects that it can almost 'rain' honeydew, a sticky substance exuded from the animals' rear ends – it takes an effort to remove it. This is an easy tree to identify, because it usually has abundant growths from the base, generally a whole network of sprouting branches, making it look messy, or even unhealthy. The Common Lime is a hybrid between two native limes, the Small-leaved and Large-leaved Limes (pp. 140 and 144). It is rare in the wild, but abundantly planted along roads and avenues. It is a tall, deciduous tree with a domed top, and dense twiggy shoots and suckers at the base, usually to 46m in height.

tree clothed from head to toe →

ABOVE & LEFT: *THE TREE IN WINTER AND SUMMER*

 Identified by the leaves, flowers, fruits, twigs and buds.
LEAVES Flat, flimsy and heart shaped, like those of other limes. They have white (not reddish) tufts on the vein lines underneath (see Small-leaved Lime), and are 6–9cm long. **FLOWERS** Hanging, heavily scented clusters of 4–10 yellowish, five-petalled flowers. Each cluster hangs down below the foliage (see Small-leaved Lime). **FRUITS** Simple round nuts (drupes), less than 1cm across, attached to a leafy bract, which gives them extra aerodynamic clout when they fall. **TWIGS** Distinctive in winter, zigzagging and bright red. Hairless (see Small-leaved Lime). **BUDS** Plump and look like 'boxing gloves', with one big and one small scale. They are 4–7mm across. **BARK** Grey-brown and closely ridged.

ABOVE LEFT: *SUMPTUOUS, HEART-SHAPED LEAVES WITH SHARP TIP*

ABOVE RIGHT: *BUDS WITH ONE LARGE SCALE AND ONE SMALL*

BELOW: *CLOSELY RIDGED BARK*

 Male and female parts are on the same flower. **SEEDS** 1–2 per nut, attached to leafy bract that propels them in the air. **FLOWERS** Insect pollinated. **LONGEVITY** To about 400 years.

 The wood is often used for piano keys.

 The leaves can be eaten raw by humans.

FACT FILE

FAMILY Malvaceae (Mallows) **HEIGHT** Maximum 50m **SIMILAR SPECIES** Other limes.

JAN	FEB	MAR	APR	MAY	JUN	JUL	AUG	SEP	OCT	NOV	DEC

LARGE-LEAVED LIME

Tilia platyphyllos

Woods on base-rich soils, especially lime. Also very often planted in parks and gardens.

This species is a large, tall deciduous tree with a domed crown, growing to 42m tall. It sounds as though it is easy to distinguish it from the closely related Small-leaved Lime (p. 140). One has larger leaves than the other! But this is a less obvious distinction than it might appear, and the best way to tell them apart is to compare the midsummer blooms – the flower spikes hang below the foliage in this species and point upwards in the Small-leaved Lime. This is a rare species in the wild in Britain, much more common in continental Europe, but both species are planted everywhere, especially to make avenues of shapely trees.

Identified by the leaves, flowers, fruits, twigs and buds.
LEAVES Heart shaped, flat, sharply toothed and bulge more on one side than the other, as in all limes. Leaves 6–9cm long (see Small-leaved Lime, 3–6cm long); occasionally up to 15cm. Veins very prominent. No obvious tufts of hairs on the leaf veins underneath (see Small-leaved Lime). **FLOWERS** In clusters (cymes) of five-petalled,

BELOW LEFT: *SMALL CLUSTERS OF FLOWERS*

BELOW RIGHT: *FLOWER CLUSTERS HANG DOWNWARDS*

FACT FILE

FAMILY Malvaceae (Mallows) HEIGHT Maximum 42m SIMILAR SPECIES Other limes.

BELOW & RIGHT: *THE TREE IN WINTER AND SUMMER*

wan yellow flowers – usually only 3–5 flowers, so fewer than in the Small-leaved Lime. Each cluster's stalk joins partway down a large, leaf-like bract, which looks like a tongue. In this species the clusters hang downwards below the foliage (upwards and above in the Small-leaved Lime). Stamens as long as petals. **FRUITS** Small, round nuts (drupes), less than 1cm long, ridged. They fall in autumn, still attached to the bract, which propels them. **TWIGS** Distinctive in winter, zigzagging and bright red. Hairy (see other limes). **BUDS** Plump and look like 'boxing gloves', with one big and one small scale. They are each 6–10mm across. **BARK** Smooth, grey (darker than the Small-leaved Lime's) and narrowly ridged, usually without bosses. Branches sinuous. Usually no sprouts at base of trunk (see Common Lime, p. 142).

ABOVE: *GREYISH BARK WITH NEAT RIDGES*

 Male and female parts occur on the same flower. **SEEDS** 1–2 per nut, attached to leafy bract that propels them in the air. **FLOWERS** Insect pollinated. **LONGEVITY** Usually up to 400 years.

 Fibres from the inner bark were once used for rope and clothing.

 The Large-leaved Lime produces the richest source of nectar for insects of any of the limes.

| JAN | FEB | MAR | APR | MAY | JUN | JUL | AUG | SEP | OCT | NOV | DEC |

COMMON ASH

Fraxinus excelsior

Almost anywhere except dunes and sandy habitat.

A large, open and slender deciduous tree, rarely exceeding 30m in height, the Common Ash is the quiet hero of the region's landscape, appearing almost anywhere, in hedgerows and fields, and along riverbanks. Its open, delicate canopy sways elegantly on breezy days. A pioneer species, it is often found in large stands of younger trees, a popular location for rookeries. The species is currently embroiled in a long battle with *Hymenoscyphus fraxineus*, a pathogenic fungus that causes ash dieback and has been decimating populations for several decades. There is currently no known cure; younger and coppiced trees are most commonly affected, whereas larger veteran trees are more resilient to the effects of the fungus.

 Can resemble other species such as the Rowan (p. 102), but the black terminal buds are unmistakable, as are the spring flowers. **FRUITS** Large bunches called keys – similar to straightened Sycamore (p. 122) fruits – in late summer, first green, then drying brown before dispersing on the wind. **LEAVES** Arranged in opposite pairs up to 40cm long, usually comprising 3–6 pairs of leaflets with a single terminal leaflet. Leaflets up to 10cm long. Each leaflet is narrowly elliptic with a serrated margin; dark green above with a paler underside. The Common Ash is one of the last trees to come into leaf in spring,

BELOW LEFT: *UNUSUAL PINNATE LEAVES*

BELOW CENTRE: *FEMALE FLOWERS*

BELOW RIGHT: *NEW AND OLD SEEDS (KEYS)*

FACT FILE

FAMILY Oleaceae (Olives & Lilacs) HEIGHT Maximum 30m SIMILAR SPECIES Veteran specimens can resemble oaks (pp. 74–79).

BELOW & RIGHT: *THE TREE IN WINTER AND SUMMER*

open canopy

around May. **FLOWERS** Develop as gnarly, deep purple knobbles that, in females, sprout into loose panicles, not unlike stem broccoli, each 5–10cm long. **BARK** Pale grey, developing shallow, broken ridges with age (smooth when young). **BUDS** Medium sized, black and arranged in opposite pairs along a stem, with a larger terminal bud.

 This tree can be dioecious or hermaphroditic. **SEEDS** Dispersed by wind. **LONGEVITY** To about 300 years, though ash dieback is significantly impacting longevity.

The wood is very straight grained and highly shock absorbent, and is used to make tool handles and furniture. It seasons quickly and is a favoured fuel for fires and log burners, burning easily even when green.

Ash trees are home to a large number of insect types, including moths, sawflies, leafhoppers and gall midges.

ABOVE LEFT: *PALE GREY BARK*

ABOVE: *DISTINCTIVE BUD WITH CHARCOAL-COLOURED TIP*

JAN	FEB	MAR	APR	MAY	JUN	JUL	AUG	SEP	OCT	NOV	DEC

WILD PRIVET

Ligustrum vulgare

Scrub and hedges, usually on-alkaline soils. Native.

RIGHT: *LEATHERY LEAVES SOMETIMES RETAINED IN WINTER*

BELOW: *IVORY-WHITE FLOWER SPIKES*

It seems destiny for an evergreen shrub – even a semi-evergreen one like the Privet – to find itself used as a hedge, and this indeed has been the fate of this attractive plant. These days it is usually replaced by the Garden Privet *L. ovalifolium*, which has broader leaves. The flower spikes give off a pleasant, sweet odour, less powerful than that of the Garden Privet. In winter, some leaves are retained and photosynthesize, while others are dropped in autumn – hence, semi-evergreen. The Wild Privet is a strongly branched, erect shrub, usually to 4m tall.

Check the leaves, flower spikes and black fruits in autumn. **LEAVES** Dull and leathery, and can look plastic. They are untoothed and occur in opposite pairs along the stem, are 3–6cm long, and although oval, are much longer than leaves of the Box (p. 134). They sometimes turn bronze without falling. **FLOWERS** Showy, in ivory-white spikes, a sort of midsummer blossom. Flowers each have four petals and are 4–5mm across. **FRUITS** Shiny black berries in billiard-ball clusters, about the size of rabbit droppings (6–8mm across). **TWIGS** Straight and round. **BARK** Reddish-brown.

Male and female flowers are on different plants. **SEEDS** 1–4 in each berry. **LONGEVITY** 20–40 years.

densely branched

FACT FILE

FAMILY Oleaceae (Olive & Ashes) HEIGHT Maximum 5m SIMILAR SPECIES Box.

JAN	FEB	MAR	APR	MAY	JUN	JUL	AUG	SEP	OCT	NOV	DEC

LILAC

Syringa vulgaris

opulent colours

The glorious flowers of the Lilac naturally decorate the rocky hillsides of south-east Europe, but their colour and scent are so admired that they have spread to gardens all over the world. They do well in the region, and are often encountered in unexpected places,

Mainly found in parks and gardens; sometimes planted in hedges and on waste ground. From southern Europe.

such as hedges and the sides of railways, or derelict houses. The shrub spreads mainly by suckering vigorously. It is a large, deciduous, multi-stemmed shrub or small tree, growing to 7m tall.

The flowers are unmistakable. **FLOWERS** In glorious, crowded clusters of colourful blooms overflowing with scent. They are up to 1.4cm long, with four petals, and may be white as well as lilac. The clusters are up to 18cm long. **LEAVES** Sumptuous, smooth, rich green, tropical looking, more or less heart shaped, and arranged in opposite pairs on the stem. They are about 10cm long and up to 8cm broad. **FRUITS** Dry brown, oval-shaped capsules 1–2cm long. **BARK** Greyish, usually smooth. **TRUNK** Bole is short.

Male and female occur in the same flower. **SEEDS** Within capsules, winged and wind dispersed. **FLOWERS** Insect pollinated. **LONGEVITY** 25–50 years or more.

Mainly as an ornamental for the eyes and nose.

The blooms are edible and excellent with honey.

ABOVE: *SMOOTH SOFT LEAVES*

BELOW: *FLOWER SPIKE*

FACT FILE

FAMILY Oleaceae (Olives & Lilacs) **HEIGHT** Maximum 7m **SIMILAR SPECIES** None.

JAN	FEB	MAR	APR	MAY	JUN	JUL	AUG	SEP	OCT	NOV	DEC

OLIVE

Olea europaea

Planted in some parts of the area, thriving only in warmer gardens and parks.

You normally see an Olive tree with the sun on your back. Few other plants are so evocative of the Mediterranean and other warm places. It is commonly planted and can thrive in the region, and many people will be familiar with it from their holidays. It is a low evergreen tree with a gnarled trunk and thick, narrow-leaved foliage, producing heavenly fruits – a feelgood tree indeed.

 Easily identified by its leaves, trunk and fruits. The flowers are small and white. **LEAVES** Evergreen, leathery, greyish-green and narrow, silvery beneath, each opposite a counterpart along the stem. They are up to 10cm long and 2cm wide. Eucalyptus (p. 90) leaves are vaguely similar but hang down and are not straight. **TRUNK** Grey and very gnarled and becomes twisted with age. **FRUITS** Olives (technically drupes), 6–15mm long, green in first year, then turn black or brown. **FLOWERS** Small, white, in hanging spikes from bases of leaves; 6–8.5mm across, with four corolla lobes.

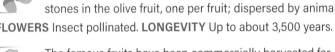 Male and female parts are on each flower. **SEEDS** The stones in the olive fruit, one per fruit; dispersed by animals. **FLOWERS** Insect pollinated. **LONGEVITY** Up to about 3,500 years.

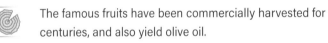 The famous fruits have been commercially harvested for centuries, and also yield olive oil.

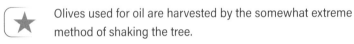 Olives used for oil are harvested by the somewhat extreme method of shaking the tree.

FACT FILE

FAMILY Oleaceae (Olives & Lilacs) HEIGHT Maximum 15m SIMILAR SPECIES Eucalyptus.

JAN	FEB	MAR	APR	MAY	JUN	JUL	AUG	SEP	OCT	NOV	DEC

ELDER

Sambucus nigra

Widespread; colonizes field and woodland margins, hedgerows and brownfield sites, as well as gardens and parks.

It may not be the tidiest looking tree, or the most elegant, but the Elder certainly has woven its way into our collective psyches for its magical associations and sheer usefulness. The tree was used by the ancient Britons to ward off evil spirits, and the leaves, thought to repel insects, were hung outside the doors of Celtic homes. The name 'Elder' purportedly comes from the old English word '*æld*', meaning 'fire', on account of the hollowed out Elder stems making handy bellows for Anglo-Saxon fires. Or it may come from the Scandinavian tree spirit Hylde-Moer; we will probably never know for sure. The Elder is a small to medium-sized, sparsely branched deciduous tree, to 15m tall.

BELOW LEFT: *UNUSUAL, BRANCHED (PINNATE) LEAVES*

BELOW RIGHT: *THE CREAM FLOWERHEADS ARE EDIBLE*

 Tricky in winter, but the early leaves are indicative; the flowers and berries are unmistakable. **LEAVES** Pinnate, opposite with 5–7 leaflets. Leaflets ovate with toothed margins; matt green, 3–7cm long. **FLOWERS** Numerous nebulous cymes of tiny, creamy-white

FACT FILE

FAMILY Adoxaceae (Moschatels) HEIGHT Maximum 15m SIMILAR SPECIES Other species in the *Sambucus* genus.

inflorescences in late spring. **BUDS** Large and ragged looking; reddish-purple and opposite on shoots. **FRUITS** Panicles of small green berries, turning deep purple and shiny; eaten by numerous animals. The berries must be handled with care, however; raw berries are toxic to humans and must be cooked before consumption. **BARK** Rugged and corky with vertical grooves and ridges; greyish in colour.

 Male and female parts are on the same tree. **SEEDS** Contained in fruits, dispersed by birds and mammals. **FLOWERS** Insect pollinated. **LONGEVITY** Up to 60 years.

untidy looking tree without many branches

BELOW LEFT: *CLUSTERS OF BLACK BERRIES*

BELOW: *TRUNK WITH VERTICAL RIDGES*

 The flowers are used to make elderflower cordial, a fruity syrup that is delicious when diluted with water; also used to flavour traditional Italian Sambuca. The berries are used as a traditional textile dye. The stems can easily be hollowed out to make whistles, bellows and other tubular tools, and the wood is particularly good for carving and whittling.

 Due to yeasts present in them, Elder flowers can be fermented into wine and even elderflower 'champagne'.

JAN	FEB	MAR	APR	MAY	JUN	JUL	AUG	SEP	OCT	NOV	DEC

GUELDER ROSE

Viburnum opulus

Woodland, scrub and hedges, especially on moist, neutral soils. Common.

The Guelder Rose is a deciduous shrub that does shrubby things exceptionally well, producing big, conspicuous, showy blooms in midsummer and equally magnificent clumps of berries in autumn and winter, not to mention some splendid leaf colour. The peculiar English name comes from the province of Gelderland in the Netherlands, and this plant is not in the rose family either, but is actually related to honeysuckles *Lonicera* spp. It is common and widespread, thriving especially in damp woodland, and growing to 4m in height.

The clusters of flowers are unique, while the berries and leaves are useful for identification. **FLOWERS** No other native tree or shrub has the little-and-large arrangement of large

small but bountiful shrub

BELOW: *THREE-LOBED LEAVES*

ABOVE & LEFT: *THE TREE IN WINTER AND SUMMER*

white flowers on the outside making a ring around very small flowers on the inside – similar to some hydrangeas. Flowerheads are also fragrant. Outer flowers 15–20mm diameter, small inner flowers 5–6mm. **FRUITS** In delicious-looking, mini-grape-like clusters of shiny red berries (technically drupes), 8–11mm across, which nestle among the reddening leaves of autumn. **LEAVES** Maple-like, deeply cut into three lobes, and with teeth. Opposite. Up to 8cm long. **BUDS** In opposite pairs, plump and red-green, like pomegranates. Terminal buds often missing. **BARK** Insipid pale grey-brown.

Flowers are both male and female. **SEEDS** A single one inside each berry. **FLOWERS** Outer flowers sterile and exist merely to attract pollinators (insects) by being showy. Inner flowers fertile and bear pollen, but not nectar. **LONGEVITY** Up to 50 years.

Best as an ornamental, although you can make jelly from the berries.

The berries are firmly attached to their stalks until December, and only then do they become easy to pluck for birds.

ABOVE LEFT: *PALE GREY-BROWN BARK*

ABOVE CENTRE: *LARGE FLOWERS IN RING OUTSIDE SMALL*

ABOVE RIGHT: *RED BERRY CLUSTERS*

BELOW LEFT: *STUNNING AUTUMN COLOUR*

BELOW: *BUDS IN OPPOSITE PAIRS*

FACT FILE

FAMILY Adoxaceae (Moschatels) HEIGHT Maximum 4m SIMILAR SPECIES Elder and Wayfaring Tree (pp. 152 and 156). Other trees with white flowers include hawthorns.

JAN	FEB	MAR	APR	MAY	JUN	JUL	AUG	SEP	OCT	NOV	DEC

WAYFARING TREE

Viburnum lantana

This deciduous shrub, usually to 5m tall, is delightfully named for its habit of growing by paths, or waysides. It is an easily overlooked shrub that blends in with the surrounding vegetation, is particularly associated with warm, chalky places and is fairly localized. However, the fashion for planting authentic native shrubs in car parks and around new builds has given it a new lease of life, enabling people to enjoy the lily-scented flowers and bicoloured berries.

Woodland edges, scrub and edges of paths. Native and southern. Widely planted.

The easiest identification clues are the distinctive fruits and very unusual buds. The leaves, flowers and twigs are also worth a look. **FRUITS** Berries (drupes) in clusters that usually exhibit two colours. They start red and turn black, though not at the same time, and are 8mm long. **BUDS** Velvety and softly hairy, with two 'ears' or angel wings. **LEAVES** Distinctly oval, wrinkled and with tiny teeth, 5–10cm long. They are downy below, and are in opposite pairs on the stem. **FLOWERS** In flat-topped clusters (cymes) 4–10cm across, creamy-white blooms, 5mm in diameter, with five petals, all the same size (see Guelder Rose p. 154) 5mm across. They have a sickly smell.

BELOW LEFT:
*FLOWERHEAD, FLOWERS
ALL THE SAME SIZE*

BELOW RIGHT:
*DIAGNOSTIC TWO-
COLOURED BERRIES*

FACT FILE

FAMILY Adoxaceae (Moschatels) HEIGHT Maximum 6m SIMILAR SPECIES Guelder Rose, Common Hawthorn and Elder (pp. 92 and 152).

BELOW: *BROWNISH-GREY SMOOTH BARK*

covered with flowerheads in summer

TWIGS Pale brown and downy. **BARK** Brownish-grey and smooth.

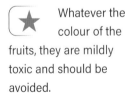 Male and female parts are within the same flower. **SEEDS** Single seed inside each berry, dispersed by birds and mammals. **FLOWERS** Insect pollinated. **LONGEVITY** Up to 50 years.

A very common ornamental often used as a native in amenity plantings.

Whatever the colour of the fruits, they are mildly toxic and should be avoided.

BELOW LEFT: *TOP SIDE OF LEAF, WRINKLED WITH TINY TEETH*

BELOW RIGHT: *DOWNY UNDERSIDE OF LEAF*

FURTHER INFORMATION

Bibliography

Bennett, R. & Bennett, N. 2022. *Tree-spotting: A Simple Guide to Britain's Trees*. Welbeck.

Blamey, M., Fitter, R. & Fitter, A. 2003. *Wild Flowers of Britain and Ireland*. A & C Black Publishers Ltd.

Fitter, R., Fitter A. & Blamey, M. 1996. *Collins Pocket Guide: Wild Flowers of Britain & Northern Europe*. HarperCollins Publishers Ltd.

Harrap, S. 2018. *Harrap's Wild Flowers: A Field Guide to the Wild Flowers of Britain & Ireland*. Bloomsbury Wildlife.

Johnson, O. & More, D. 2015. *Collins British Tree Guide*. William Collins.

Johnson, O. & More, D. 2006. *Collins Tree Guide*. William Collins.

Mabey, R. 1996. *Flora Britannica*. Sinclair-Stevenson.

Mossberg, B. and Stenberg, L. 2015. *Fjällflora*. Wahlström & Widstrand.

Peterken, G. 2023. *Trees and Woodlands. British Wildlife Collection No 12*. Bloomsbury Wildlife.

Poland, J. 2018. *The Field Key to Winter Twigs*. Botanical Society of Britain and Ireland.

Price, D. & Bersweden, L. (No date). *Winter Trees: A Photographic Guide to Common Trees and Shrubs*. Field Studies Council Publications.

Rushforth, K. 1996. *Mitchell Beazley Pocket Guide to Trees*. Mitchell Beazley.

Stace, C. 2010. *New Flora of the British Isles*, 3rd edition. Cambridge University Press.

Sterry, P. 2008. *Collins Complete Guide to British Trees.* HarperCollins Publishers Ltd.

Thomas, P. A. 2022. *The New Naturalist Library: Trees*. William Collins.

Useful Organisations and Websites

Botanical Society of Britain & Ireland: https://bsbi.org

Natural History Museum Tree Guide: www.nhm.ac.uk/take-part/identify-nature/uk-tree-identification-guide.html

Royal Horticultural Society: www.rhs.org.uk

The Tree Council: www.treecouncil.org.uk

Tree and Flower Identification Guide: www.treeguideuk.co.uk

Woodland Trust: www.woodlandtrust.org.uk

World Flora Online Plant List: www.theplantlist.org

Authors' Websites

Dominic Couzens www.birdwords.co.uk

Gail Ashton www.gailashton.co.uk

Identification Apps

iNaturalist

iPlant

Leafsnap

PictureThis

Plantnet

TreeID

INDEX OF COMMON NAMES

Tick boxes are included next to the English name of each species so you can mark off species that you have seen.

☐ Alder Buckthorn 135
☐ Apple 100
☐ Aspen 54
☐ Austrian Pine 35

☐ Bay 87
☐ Bird Cherry 116
☐ Black Mulberry 84
☐ Black Poplar 49
☐ Blackthorn 112
☐ Bog Myrtle 56
☐ Box 134

☐ Cedar of Lebanon 24
☐ Cherry Plum 111
☐ Cherry Laurel 117
☐ Common Alder 64
☐ Common Ash 147
☐ Common Beech 70
☐ Common Hawthorn 92
☐ Common Hazel 68
☐ Common Juniper 20
☐ Common Laburnum 126
☐ Common Lime 142
☐ Common Walnut 56
☐ Common Whitebeam 104
☐ Corsican Pine 36
☐ Crab Apple 98
☐ Crack Willow 38

☐ Dogwood 132
☐ Douglas Fir 32
☐ Downy Birch 62
☐ Dwarf Willow 45

☐ Elder 152
☐ Eucalyptus 90
☐ European Larch 28
☐ European Silver Fir 26
☐ Evergreen Oak 78

☐ Field Elm 82
☐ Field Maple 118

☐ Giant Sequoia 22
☐ Goat Willow 44
☐ Grey Alder 63
☐ Grey Poplar 49
☐ Grey Willow 43
☐ Guelder Rose 154

☐ Holly 128
☐ Hornbeam 66
☐ Horse Chestnut 124
☐ Hybrid Black Poplar 50

☐ Italian Cypress 19

☐ Japanese Larch 29

☐ Large-leaved Lime 144
☐ Lawson's Cypress 18
☐ Leyland Cypress 19
☐ Lilac 149
☐ Lombardy Poplar 52
☐ London Plane 88

☐ Magnolia 85
☐ Maidenhair Tree 12
☐ Midland Hawthorn 94
☐ Monkey Puzzle 14

☐ Norway Maple 120
☐ Norway Spruce 30

☐ Olive 150
☐ Osier 42

☐ Pedunculate Oak 74
☐ Purging Buckthorn 136

☐ Rhododendron 127
☐ Rowan 102

☐ Scots Pine 34
☐ Sea Buckthorn 138
☐ Sessile Oak 76
☐ Silver Birch 60
☐ Sitka Spruce 31
☐ Small-leaved Lime 140
☐ Spindle 130
☐ Stone Pine 37
☐ Swedish Whitebeam 108
☐ Sweet Chestnut 72
☐ Sycamore 123

☐ True Wild Pear 97
☐ Tulip Tree 86

☐ Turkey Oak 79

☐ Wayfaring Tree 156
☐ Weeping Willow 40
☐ White Poplar 46
☐ White Willow 39
☐ Wild Cherry 114
☐ Wild Pear 96
☐ Wild Plum 110
☐ Wild Privet 148
☐ Wild Service Tree 106
☐ Wych Elm 80

☐ Yew 16

INDEX OF SCIENTIFIC NAMES

Abies alba 26
Acer campestre 118
   platanoides 120
   pseudoplatanus 122
Aesculus hippocastanum 124
Alnus glutinosa 64
   incana 63
Araucaria araucana 14

Betula pubescens 62
   pendula 60
Buxus sempervirens 134

Carpinus betulus 66
Castanea sativa 72
Cedrus libani 25
Cornus sanguinea 132
Corylus avellana 68
Crataegus laevigata 94
   monogyna 92
Cupressus x leylandii 19
   sempervirens 19

Eucalyptus spp. 90
Euonymus europaeus 130

Fagus sylvatica 70
Frangula alnus 135
Fraxinus excelsior 146

Ginkgo biloba 12

Hippophae rhamnoides 138

Ilex aquifolium 128

Juglans regia 56

Laburnum anagyroides 126
Larix decidua 28
   kaempferi 29
Laurus nobilis 87
Ligustrum vulgare 148
Liriodendron tulipifera 86

Magnolia spp. 85
Malus pumila 100
   sylvestris 98
Morus nigra 84
Myrica gale 58

Olea europaea 150

Picea abies 30
   sitchensis 31
Pinus nigra ssp. *nigra* 35
   nigra pinea 37
   sylvestris 34
Platanus x acerifolia 88
Populus alba 46
   x *canadensis* 50
   x *canescens* 48
   nigra 49
   nigra var. *italica* 52
   tremula 54
Prunus Avium 114
   cerasifera 111
   domestica 110
   laurocerasus 117
   padus 116
   spinosa 112
Pseudotsuga menziesii 32

Pyrus communis 96
   pyraster 97

Quercus cerris 79
   ilex 78
   petraea 76
   robur 74

Rhamnus cathartica 136
Rhododendron ponticum 127

Salix alba 39
   capraea 44
   cinerea 43
   x *fragilis* 38
   herbacea 45
   x *sepulchralis* 40
   viminalis 42
Sambucus nigra 152
Sorbus aria 104
   aucuparia 102
   intermedia 108
   torminalis 106
Syringa vulgari 149

Taxus baccata 16
Tilia cordata 140
   x *europaea* 142
   platyphyllos 144

Ulmus glabra 81
   minor 82

Viburnum lantana 156
   opulus 154

Acknowledgements

Dominic Couzens and Gail Ashton wish to thank John Beaufoy for agreeing to do the book, Rosemary Wilkinson for getting it all together, Nigel Partridge for the design and Krystyna Mayer for the editing. What a great team. Dominic sends much love to his wife, Carolyn, for coping with him while he wrote the book - never easy. Gail would like to thank her friends and family for their help in hunting down so many beautiful trees to photograph in wind, rain and shine.